P9-CKX-349

P9-CKX-349

TARZAN®

THE BROADWAY ADVENTURE

JOSH STRICKLAND

MICHAEL LASSELL

DISNEY
EDITIONS
NEW YORK

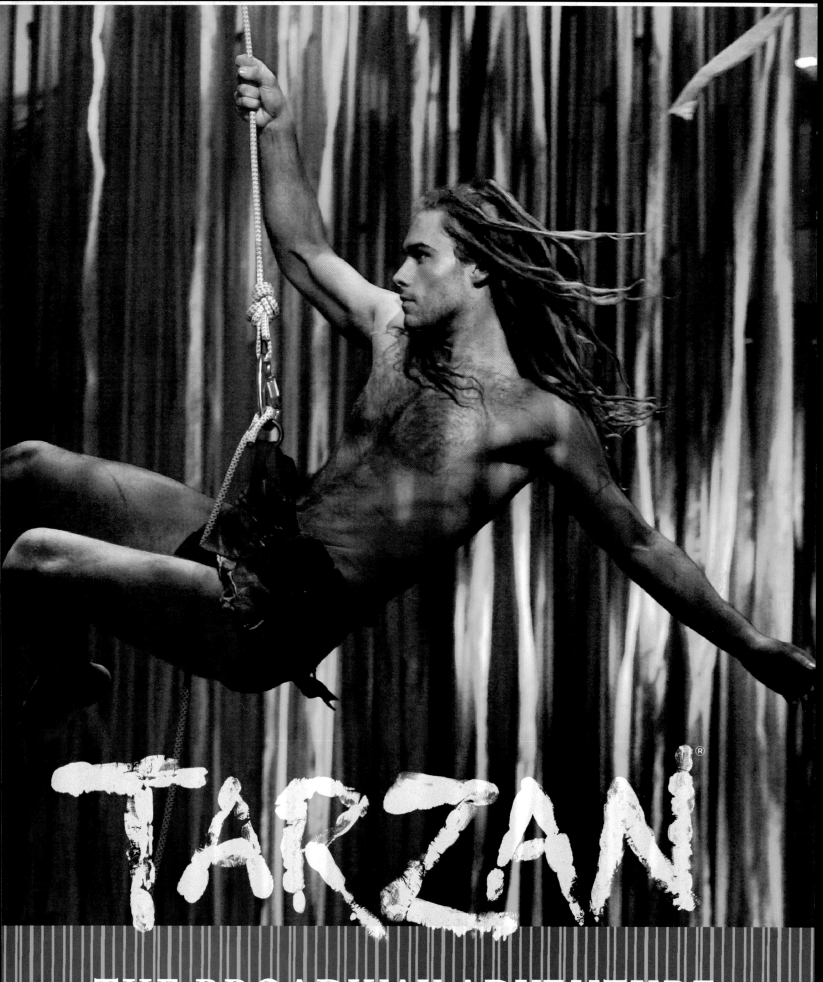

TARZAN®

THE BROADWAY ADVENTURE

DEDICATION
This book is dedicated to
every man, woman, or child
who has ever appeared in
the ensemble of a Broadway musical,

especially to the magnificent
high-flying ensemble of *Tarzan*—

and to the enormously talented and unsung
understudies, swings, and covers!

Tarzan® Owned by Edgar Rice Burroughs, Inc.
Used by Permission.
Copyright © 2007 Edgar Rice Burroughs, Inc.
and Disney Enterprises, Inc.

All rights reserved. No part of this book may be
reproduced or transmitted in any form or by any means,
electronic or mechanical, including photocopying,
recording, or by any information storage and retrieval
system, without written permission from the publisher.

Two Worlds
You'll Be in My Heart
Son of Man
Trashin' the Camp
Strangers Like Me
Lyrics by Phil Collins. Reprinted by permission.
©1998, 1999 Edgar Rice Burroughs, Inc. and Walt Disney
Music Company (ASCAP)
All Rights Reserved. Lyrics reprinted by permission.

Jungle Funk
Who Better Than Me?
No Other Way
I Need to Know
Sure As Sun Turns To Moon
Waiting for This Moment
Different
Like No Man I've Ever Seen
For the First Time
Everything That I Am
Lyrics by Phil Collins. Reprinted by permission.
©2006 Philip Collins Publishing, Ltd. (PRS)/Pentagon
Music Co. (BMI)
All Rights Reserved. Lyrics reprinted by permission.

"Academy Award," "Oscar," are registered trademarks
of the Academy of Motion Picture Arts and Sciences.

"Tony" is a registered trademark of the American Theater Wing.

"Grammy" is a registered trademark of The Recording Academy.

"Golden Globe" is a registered trademark of the
Hollywood Foreign Press Association.

"Emmy" is a registered trademark of the Academy of Television
Arts and Sciences/National Television Academy.

For information address Disney Editions,
114 Fifth Avenue, New York, New York 10011-5690.

Printed in the United States of America

First Edition
10 9 8 7 6 5 4 3 2 1

Library of Congress Cataloging-in-Publication Data on file.
ISBN-13: 978-1-4231-0085-0
ISBN-10: 1-4231-0085-9

PHOTO CREDITS:
Unless otherwise noted, TARZAN color performance and
rehearsal photography by Joan Marcus. TARZAN studio shots
(both black & white and tinted) are by Ruven Afanador.

p. 14 (bottom) and p. 17
© 1975 Edgar Rice Burroughs Inc.

pp. 14, 16, 17, 18, 19, 20, 21
Courtesy Edgar Rice Burroughs Estate.

pp. 14, 21, 29 animated images © 2007 Edgar Rice Burroughs,
Inc. and Disney Enterprises, Inc. All Rights Reserved.

pp. 24-28, 46-47 Courtesy Bob Crowley Studio

pp. 102 (top right, bottom left), 107 (bottom right)
Ivo Coveney

pp. 105 (top), 138-139 Heinz Kluetmeier

pp. 152-157 Lyn Hughes

DISNEY THEATRICAL PRODUCTIONS
under the direction of
Thomas Schumacher

presents

TARZAN®

Music and Lyrics by
PHIL COLLINS
Book by
DAVID HENRY HWANG
with

**JOSH STRICKLAND   JENN GAMBATESE
MERLE DANDRIDGE   CHESTER GREGORY II
TIM JEROME   DONNIE KESHAWARZ
DANIEL MANCHE   ALEX RUTHERFORD**
and
SHULER HENSLEY

DARRIN BAKER   MARCUS BELLAMY   CELINA CARVAJAL   DWAYNE CLARK   VERONICA deSOYZA
KEARRAN GIOVANNI   MICHAEL HOLLICK   JOSHUA KOBAK   KARA MADRID   KEVIN MASSEY
ANASTACIA McCLESKEY   RIKA OKAMOTO   MARLYN ORTIZ   WHITNEY OSENTOSKI   JOHN ELLIOTT OYZON
ANDY PELLICK   ANGELA PHILLIPS   STEFAN RAULSTON   HORACE V. ROGERS   SEAN SAMUELS
NICK SANCHEZ   NIKI SCALERA   NATALIE SILVERLIEB   JD AUBREY SMITH   RACHEL STERN

Based on the novel *Tarzan of the Apes* by
EDGAR RICE BURROUGHS
and the Disney film *Tarzan*
Screenplay by
TAB MURPHY, BOB TZUDIKER & NONI WHITE
Directed by
KEVIN LIMA & CHRIS BUCK

Scenic and Costume Design   Lighting Design
BOB CROWLEY   **NATASHA KATZ**
Sound Design   Hair Design   Make-Up Design
JOHN SHIVERS   **DAVID BRIAN BROWN**   **NAOMI DONNE**
Soundscape   Special Creatures   Fight Direction
LON BENDER   **IVO COVENEY**   **RICK SORDELET**
Vocal Arrangements   Dance Arrangements   Orchestrations
PAUL BOGAEV   **JIM ABBOTT**   **DOUG BESTERMAN**
Musice Director   Music Coordinator   Casting
JIM ABBOTT   **MICHAEL KELLER**   BERNARD **TELSEY CASTING**
Production Supervisor   Technical Supervision   Press Representative
CLIFFORD SCHWARTZ   **TOM SHANE BUSSEY**   **BONEAU/BRYAN-BROWN**
Associate Director   Associate Producer
JEFF LEE   **MARSHALL B. PURDY**

Aerial Design by
PICHÓN BALDINU
Music Produced by
PAUL BOGAEV
Choreography by
MERYL TANKARD
Direction by
BOB CROWLEY

CONTENTS

Two Worlds, Two Adventures

"Put your faith in what you most believe in—
Two worlds, one family ... "

TARZAN®, THE STAGE MUSICAL—presented by Disney Theatrical Productions—opened at the Richard Rodgers Theater in New York City on May 10, 2006. It was a mild spring evening and a festive one. Arriving guests were greeted by a battery of press photographers and a traditional red carpet, as well as a not-so-traditional carpet in the shade of green you might see if equatorial sunlight were shining on foliage just after a rainfall—the color of the show's official logo.

Across 46th Street, Disney's *Beauty and the Beast* was still running (the sixth-longest-running show in Broadway history). Actress Angela Lansbury, who was the voice of Mrs. Potts in the animated *Beauty* film, was among the celebrities on hand to welcome the "King of the Apes" to the Great White Way. Other dignitaries included Danton Burroughs, grandson of populist American writer Edgar Rice Burroughs, who created the character of Tarzan almost 100 years ago.

Inside the newly refurbished theater, 1,400 theatergoers were greeted by a proscenium arch entirely filled by an act curtain that consisted of two inky stage drops: a porous scrim superimposed on a seamless silk. On the scrim was a white outline map of Africa from the late 19th century; the silk presented a ship tossing on high seas.

Meanwhile, an elaborate sound track played wind and waves, sea birds, straining ropes, creaking planks, and the ship's bell as the merchant barque was tossed about by foul weather in the south Atlantic. Those who were reading the captain's log entries projected onto the map saw that this ship was the *Fuwalda*, that the time was the summer of 1888, and that the ship's passengers included one Lord Greystoke, his wife (Lady Alice), and their infant son.

As the motion of the scenic *Fuwalda* increased—the silky drop billowing like a ship's sails, thanks to the backstage crew, so did the volume of the sound track—until a flash of lighting and a crack of thunder pitched the theater into total darkness.

Tarzan had arrived on Broadway—more than five years in the making.

KEVIN MASSEY, CELINA CARVAJAL

A Journey of a Thousand Miles...

Broadway musicals have one opening night, but many beginnings, and *Tarzan* had more beginnings than most. The story first appeared in 1912. The first film was made in 1918. Dozens more books and movies followed, as did radio broadcasts, comic strips, television shows, and a warehouse full of merchandise bearing the image of a character who can summon elephants with a cry as familiar to our ears as the picture of the hero-in-a-loincloth is to our eyes.

But Tarzan of the Congo is not a stranger to the concrete jungle. His last visit to Gotham was in the 1942 film *Tarzan's New York Adventure*, in which star Johnny Weissmuller actually dove off the Brooklyn Bridge.

By the time Disney's animated *Tarzan* reached movie screens in 1999, the story of the little British lord who was adopted by great apes in Africa had become the second-most filmed story in the history of Hollywood (only Count Dracula has moved studios to produce more celluloid footage).

The book you hold in your hand has several purposes. It is meant to be a celebration of the show and a keepsake of the first-ever stage musical version of the *Tarzan* tale. It is also a photo album dedicated to the production. It's a record of some of the work that went on behind the scenes by a small army of creative women and men over the course of five years, to bring the story to life. It's a companion to the show, much as the bonus material on a DVD is to the theatrical version of a movie.

The book, like the Disney stage musical and the film before it, also has a theme. It's taken from the lyrics of one of the songs that the phenomenal Phil Collins wrote for the *Tarzan* movie: "Two Worlds."

PUT YOUR FAITH IN WHAT YOU MOST BELIEVE IN
TWO WORLDS, ONE FAMILY
TRUST YOUR HEART
LET FATE DECIDE
TO GUIDE THESE LIVES WE SEE

In a world of constantly warring factions, *Tarzan* is the story of two opposing camps coming together, of reconciliation, and a resolution of conflict.

This dichotomy of worlds has multiple meanings for the Disney production of *Tarzan* on Broadway. First, and most obviously, are the two worlds that the character of Tarzan inhabits, both the ape world—with his foster parents, Kala and Kerchak, and his best friend, Terk—and the world of humans, of Jane, Professor Porter, and, sadly, Clayton—which Tarzan comes to know as the world into which he was born.

The hero of the tale must put to rest the conflicts caused by his birth into one tribe and his allegiance to another, between his family of origin and the family that raised him and that he loves. These are Tarzan's two worlds, and his exploration of these two different realms—civilization and the jungle—is the title character's central adventure. This is the realm of the story's plot, of its narrative thrust.

The second adventure is the process of making a Broadway musical. And that is the adventure by which a script becomes a three-dimensional show that

KEVIN MASSEY, CELINA CARVAJAL

takes place in a theater in the course of two and a half hours of acting, singing, and dancing. The show is both a story and the means of telling the story.

"Before I put something onstage," says Thomas Schumacher, president of Disney Theatrical Productions and the producer of *The Lion King*, *Elton John and Tim Rice's Aida*, *Mary Poppins* (coproduced with Cameron Mackintosh), and all of Disney's other stage ventures around the world—"it has to have two things. First, there has to be an engaging story that serves as the basis for great music. Then I look for the extra thing: what would make staging this story fun? Without a captivating story with great characters, compelling music, and an inventive staging hook, it's not really the show for us.

"In going back to the original book," Schumacher continues, "I was struck that what made *Tarzan* a Disney story was that it centers on family, on the question of what a family is. What makes it timely, as families become more complex and more diverse, is that it looks at some of the basic questions of life, the 'Who am I?' and 'Where do I belong?' questions that can cause so much pain as we're growing up.

"*Tarzan* speaks in particular to kids who have been adopted. Or who live in blended families with stepparents and stepsiblings. Or who are physically or emotionally challenged in some way. Or just not proficient in the activities other kids may care about, like sports. It speaks to anyone who has ever felt abandoned, rejected, or misunderstood. And it's about the power of family— sometimes the family we're born into, sometimes the family that takes us in, sometimes the family we create to heal that sense of isolation and alienation. It's about what it means to be a social being.

"So we hoped that with *Tarzan* we had our sights trained on a rousing good yarn with serious intellectual undercurrents that would appeal to a family audience. We already had the beginnings of a great score with Phil Collins's music for the film. But how would we tell this story? And how would we tell it onstage?"

In fact, the development of *Tarzan*, from the idea of a stage production to its final incarnation at the Richard Rodgers Theater was long and complex, but some elements never changed. In particular, the creative personnel assembled to develop the show for its initial run.

The story of *Tarzan* on Broadway is one of collaboration on a global scale. The director as well as designer of the show, Bob Crowley, who was born in Ireland, became known for his decades of work in the major theaters of England; Phil Collins, the composer, is an international music star from the U.K., who lives in Switzerland and New York. Choreographer Meryl Tankard hails from Australia but spent an important segment of her career working in Germany, and the flying master, Pichón Baldinu, lives and works in his native Argentina. The book writer, David Henry Hwang, has taken as the central theme of his work his own two worlds as the American-born son of immigrants from China.

Cast members come from all over the United States, as well as Canada and Japan, and celebrate the great diversity that makes the United States unique among nations. And in this very real sense, the making of *Tarzan* represents the extent to which human beings of vastly divergent cultural and aesthetic experiences can come together to make art.

After they are shipwrecked off the coast of Africa, Lord and Lady Greystoke, with the infant who will grow up to be Tarzan, make their way onto the beach (shown are Kara Madrid and Michael Hollick).

BIRTH OF A JOURNEY

I

ALEX RUTHERFORD

TARZAN'S ADVENTURE BEGINS

IN THE DISNEY ANIMATED *TARZAN*", as well as the stage musical, Tarzan's birth father, Lord Greystoke of England, is killed by a leopard (as is his mother) after the family survives a shipwreck on the coast of Africa. As he grows up, young Tarzan is frequently at odds with Kerchak, the silverback gorilla who is the head of the family group Tarzan inhabits, thanks to Kala, his ape mother who adopts him. A great deal of Tarzan's unhappiness comes from his relationship, or lack of one, with Kerchak.

But in a very real sense, Tarzan had an even earlier father: Edgar Rice Burroughs, from whose imagination Tarzan sprang fully formed in 1912.

Edgar Rice Burroughs was himself born in Chicago in 1875. His erratic education included bronco busting in frontier Idaho and mastering classical languages at the Phillips Academy in Andover, Massachusetts. He ultimately graduated from Michigan Military Academy and served in the U.S. Army in Arizona until he was discharged due to a heart murmur. For the next dozen years he worked in a variety of jobs—as a railway policeman, door-to-door salesman, accountant, manager of the clerical department of Sears, Roebuck & Company, and, finally, a wholesaler of pencil sharpeners.

In 1911, inspired by the popular "pulp" magazines of the day (so-named because of the inexpensive paper on which they were printed), Burroughs began to write, with no experience except for the fairy tales he had concocted for his children. It has been said that after reading a few of these pulp stories while waiting for orders for pencil sharpeners to materialize, Burroughs simply put down the magazine and said, "Well, I can certainly write this kind of stuff as well as these other fellows," or words to that effect. And his writing career began.

Burroughs's first published story, a science fiction tale entitled "Under the Moons of Mars," was serialized in *The All-Story* magazine, one of the most popular pulps, between February and July of 1912. That same magazine rejected the aspiring writer's next effort, despite the success of his debut tale (it was, however, accepted by a rival publisher). No one was prepared for the neophyte author's third published literary effort, *Tarzan of the Apes*, which was printed in full in the October 1912 issue of *The All-Story*, an unprecedented honor.

"It is the most exciting story we have seen in a blue moon, and about as original as they make 'em," wrote Thomas Metcalf, the editor of *The All-Story*. Metcalf paid Burroughs $700 for *Tarzan of the Apes*, which may not seem like much in 2006, but in 1912 it was a princely sum for a writer—in that same year a factory-fresh Model-T Ford could be bought for $695.

Why was *Tarzan* so popular? It's difficult to say, and the reasons were, perhaps, multiple. That the story told of a great adventure in what was then an exotic land is clear. And it certainly spoke to an entire generation that grew

Edgar Rice Burroughs (shown at his typewriter, BELOW) wrote two dozen books featuring Tarzan. The INSET ABOVE shows the first.

© 1975 Edgar Rice Burroughs Inc.

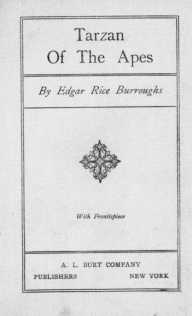

up, like Burroughs, in the years following the Civil War (a conflict in which Burroughs's father was a Union Army officer).

Africa in the late 19th century was still a continent vastly unknown to Europe and America. In fact, the United States was barely finished with its own Wild West era (one of Burroughs's assignments in the Army had been to track the remnants of the Apache Nation). The continental United States was only completed with the admission of New Mexico and Arizona into the Union in 1912. Oklahoma, the 46th state, was admitted in 1907, during the administration of Theodore Roosevelt, a man known as "Old Rough and Ready" not only for his exploits in Cuba during the Spanish-American War of 1898 but also for his big-game hunting safaris in Africa. Sir Henry Morton Stanley had only located David Livingstone ("Dr. Livingstone, I presume") four years before Burroughs was born.

By 1912, the world was also suffering from the effects of the Industrial Revolution, and in particular the dehumanization of the work force by the assembly line and mechanical reproduction. There was a widespread nostalgia for the early 19th-century days of the rugged individual, the man of action, of the craftsman and artisan. Tarzan, clearly, existed in a world outside of the city realities of most of the story's readers: long workdays, low wages, crowded tenement conditions, and a growing sense of the expendability of the individual.

So the story of Tarzan was very much of its time. Its continued success seems to be inherent in the story and the echoes it taps into of the yearning even the most civilized among us feels to go back to nature and, in so doing, to recapture some of what has been lost or sacrificed in the process of modernization. Ironically, it is the "uncivilized" Tarzan who behaves in the most civilized manner, which is partly a testimony to his character and partly the notion of Edgar Rice Burroughs that human nobility will always win out over greed, sin, and excess (the "animal" traits that exist, paradoxically, only in man). Tarzan is a force for good in a world in which evil lurks in many forms.

In any case, the success of *Tarzan* was immediate and enormous. Burroughs went on to write another 25 books about the young English lord who was raised by Congo apes—as well as dozens of other books, including numerous futurist fantasies. Edgar Rice Burroughs is, in fact, considered by many not only to be the father of Tarzan but of American science fiction, too.

The first Tarzan film, *Tarzan of the Apes,* starring Elmo Lincoln, was made in 1917, with the bayous of Louisiana standing in for Africa. The apes were played by young male members of the New Orleans Athletic Club, and the costumes were so hot that shooting could only proceed at a snail's pace between cool-off periods. To call the costumes "unconvincing" would be generous.

When the film debuted in 1918 credit was given to Elmo Lincoln for playing Tarzan (Gordon Griffith played Young Tarzan), but the film's shooting had begun with a Swedish lead actor named Stellan Windrow, who had completed all the vine swinging and aerial stunts before he was drafted into the U.S. Navy. His replacement, Elmo Lincoln, it turned out, was deathly afraid of heights, so all the tree-hopping in the film is Windrow's.

The 55-minute silent film was as big a hit as the original magazine story. It was one of the first movies to earn over $1 million despite Burroughs's misgivings about the 30-year-old star: "Elmo was a huge, barrel-chested man," Burroughs later wrote, "who looked like he could knock a tree over instead of swinging from one."

Since 1918, "The King of the Jungle," as he came to be called, has appeared in virtually every medium, from newspaper comic strips to radio and television. Burroughs's daughter Joan, who voiced the role of Jane in several radio serials in the 1930s, even married one of the silver screen's Tarzans, Jim Pierce.

The Burroughs ranch, in the San Fernando Valley, near Los Angeles, lent its name to the town that grew up around it—Tarzana (from which the Edgar Rice Burroughs estate is still administered, by Danton Burroughs, the writer's grandson). Only one screen Tarzan ever lived in Tarzana: Lex Baker, who played the role in five films between 1949 and 1953, including 1951's *Tarzan's Peril*, the first to actually shoot in Africa.

By the time he died in 1950, Edgar Rice Burroughs was wealthy, famous, powerful, and respected. He had wanted to create popular entertainment, and his heroic orphan boy was already one of the most popular and admired literary characters of all time.

Chicago-born Burroughs (OPPOSITE) built his estate, Tarzana, in the San Fernando Valley (BELOW LEFT). Elmo Lincoln as Tarzan in 1918 (left).

The Edgar Rice Burroughs Tarzan Bookshelf

Tarzan of the Apes

The Return of Tarzan

Beasts of Tarzan

Son of Tarzan

Tarzan and the Jewels of Opar

Jungle Tales of Tarzan

Tarzan the Untamed

Tarzan the Terrible

Tarzan and the Golden Lion

Tarzan and the Antmen

Tarzan, Lord of the Jungle

Tarzan and the Lost Empire

Tarzan at the Earth's Core

Tarzan the Invincible

Tarzan Triumphant

Tarzan and the City of Gold

Tarzan and the Lionman

Tarzan and the Leopard Men

Tarzan's Quest

Tarzan and the Forbidden City

Tarzan the Magnificent

Tarzan and the Foreign Legion

Tarzan and the Madman

Tarzan and the Champion

Tarzan and the Jungle Murders

Tarzan and the Castaways

Tarzan and the Tarzan Twins

Tarzan: The Lost Adventure

IN SEARCH OF TARZAN

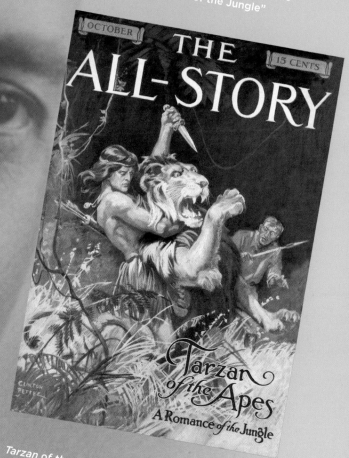

1875   Edgar Rice Burroughs, creator of Tarzan, born in Chicago

1911   Burroughs's first story published, in *The All-Story* magazine: "Under the Moon of Mars," a science-fiction fantasy

1912   *Tarzan of the Apes* debuts in the October issue of *The All-Story* magazine with the subtitle: "A Romance of the Jungle"

1913   *Tarzan of the Apes* serialized in American newspapers.

1914   *Tarzan of the Apes* appears in book form (current auction value of a first imprint/first edition is approximately $50,000).

1917   The first film, *Tarzan of the Apes,* shoots in Louisiana with young male members of the New Orleans Athletic Club playing the apes.

1918   The debut of *Tarzan of the Apes,* the first Tarzan film.

EDGAR RICE BURROUGHS

© 1975 Edgar Rice Burroughs Inc.

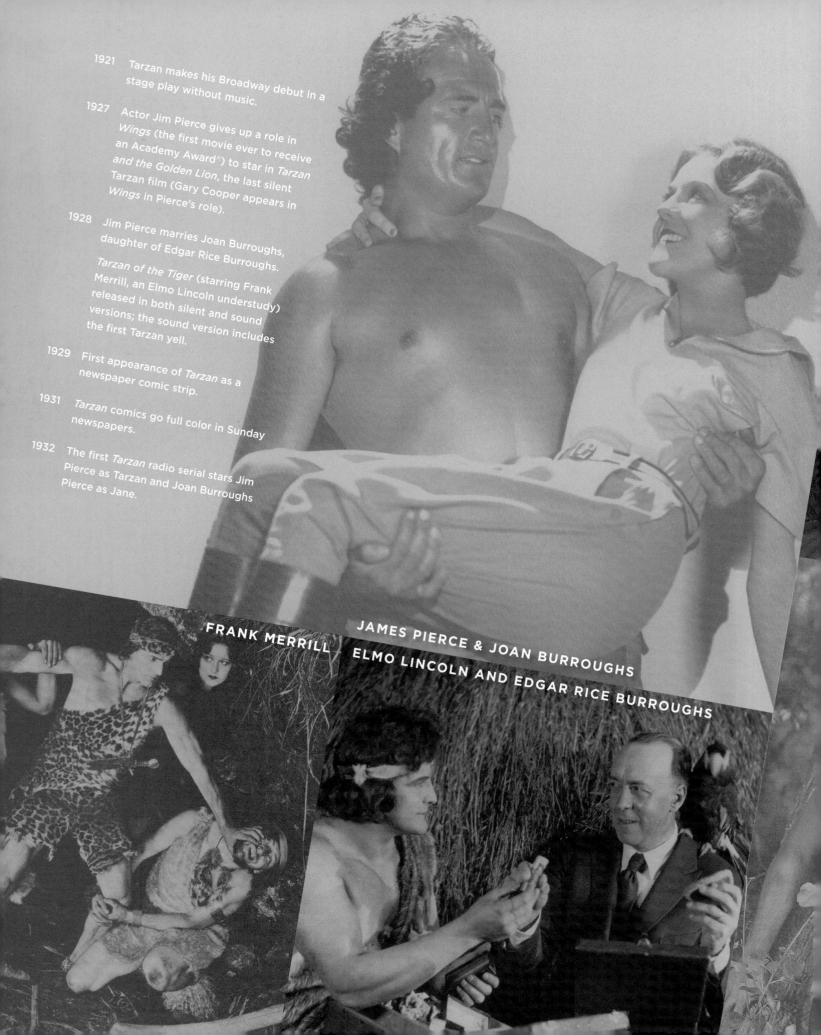

1921 Tarzan makes his Broadway debut in a stage play without music.

1927 Actor Jim Pierce gives up a role in *Wings* (the first movie ever to receive an Academy Award®) to star in *Tarzan and the Golden Lion*, the last silent Tarzan film (Gary Cooper appears in *Wings* in Pierce's role).

1928 Jim Pierce marries Joan Burroughs, daughter of Edgar Rice Burroughs.

Tarzan of the Tiger (starring Frank Merrill, an Elmo Lincoln understudy) released in both silent and sound versions; the sound version includes the first Tarzan yell.

1929 First appearance of *Tarzan* as a newspaper comic strip.

1931 Tarzan comics go full color in Sunday newspapers.

1932 The first *Tarzan* radio serial stars Jim Pierce as Tarzan and Joan Burroughs Pierce as Jane.

FRANK MERRILL

JAMES PIERCE & JOAN BURROUGHS

ELMO LINCOLN AND EDGAR RICE BURROUGHS

CHEETA, JOHNNY WEISSMULLER & MAUREEN O' SULLIVAN

BUSTER CRABBE

1932 Olympic swimming champion Johnny Weissmuller makes his first Tarzan film: *Tarzan the Ape Man*, with Maureen O'Sullivan as Jane. Shot in California and Florida, the film incorporates actual footage of Africa shot for another film.

1933 Buster Crabbe, another Olympic swimming gold medalist, stars as the Lord of the Jungle in *Tarzan the Fearless*.

1934 – 1948 The Weissmuller Years

Director John Farrow, brought in after the original director of *Tarzan Escapes* (1936) was fired, married Maureen O'Sullivan (Jane); their daughter is Mia Farrow.

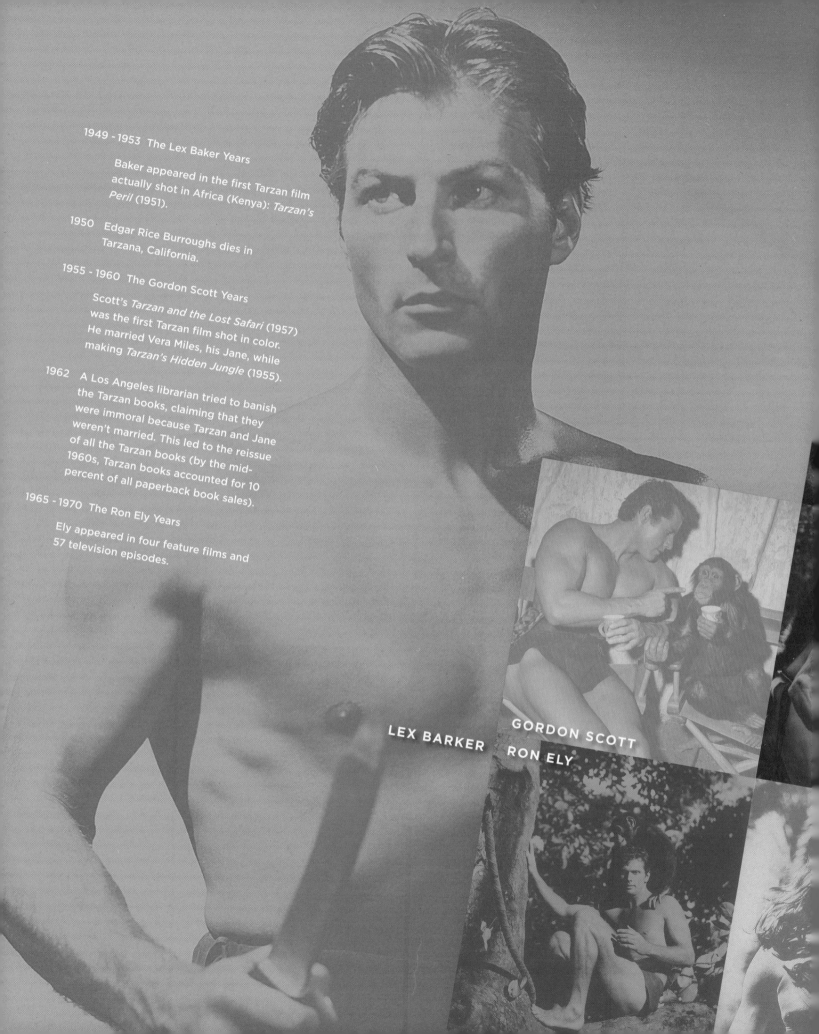

1949 - 1953 The Lex Baker Years

Baker appeared in the first Tarzan film actually shot in Africa (Kenya): *Tarzan's Peril* (1951).

1950 Edgar Rice Burroughs dies in Tarzana, California.

1955 - 1960 The Gordon Scott Years

Scott's *Tarzan and the Lost Safari* (1957) was the first Tarzan film shot in color. He married Vera Miles, his Jane, while making *Tarzan's Hidden Jungle* (1955).

1962 A Los Angeles librarian tried to banish the Tarzan books, claiming that they were immoral because Tarzan and Jane weren't married. This led to the reissue of all the Tarzan books (by the mid-1960s, Tarzan books accounted for 10 percent of all paperback book sales).

1965 - 1970 The Ron Ely Years

Ely appeared in four feature films and 57 television episodes.

LEX BARKER

GORDON SCOTT

RON ELY

1976 *Tarzan* runs as an animated television cartoon show.

1981 Miles O'Keeffe stars as the hairless he-man, with Bo Derrick as Jane (The Burroughs estate, unhappy with the portrayal of Tarzan and other matters, went to court to prevent this film from being distributed).

1984 Christopher Lambert portrays Tarzan in the well-regarded *Greystoke: The Legend of Tarzan, Lord of the Apes.*

1991-1994 Wolf Larson plays Tarzan on television (75 episodes).

1996-1997 Joe Lara stars in 22 episodes of TV's *Tarzan: The Epic Adventures.*

1998 Casper van Dien stars in *Tarzan and the Lost City.*

1999 Disney's animated feature film *Tarzan* features the voice talents of Tony Goldwyn, Minnie Driver, and Glenn Close, with music by Phil Collins. *Tarzan* becomes the fifth-ranked box-office hit of the year (*Toy Story 2* ranks 3rd).

2001-2003 Disney airs the half-hour animated series, *The Legend of Tarzan*

2002 Disney's animated *Tarzan & Jane* debuts on video.

2003-2004 WB presents an updated (and short-lived) *Tarzan,* starring underwear model Travis Fimmel.

2005 Disney releases *Tarzan II* on video.

2006 MAY 10: Disney's musical version of *Tarzan* opens live on Broadway at the Richard Rodgers Theater.

JUNE 27: *Tarzan,* the Broadway cast album, debuts.

WOLF LARSEN

CHRISTOPHER LAMBERT

CASPER VAN DIEN

JOE LARA

ANIMATED TARZAN

ONE OF THE BEGINNINGS of any theatrical production is, of course, the selection of the creative personnel—the director, designers, composer, playwright. For Disney's Thomas Schumacher, some of those choices were absolutely clear. Phil Collins would compose the music and provide the song lyrics, as he had for the animated film.

The book would be written by the Tony Award®-winning playwright of *M. Butterfly,* David Henry Hwang, who had not only worked on the Broadway book of *Elton John and Tim Rice's Aida*, but who has written numerous opera libretti and was nominated for a Tony Award for his own (nonmusical) *Golden Child* and later for his revision of Rodgers and Hammerstein's *Flower Drum Song.*

The book of the *Tarzan* musical would be based both on the original *Tarzan of the Apes* by Edgar Rice Burroughs and the Disney animated film—screenplay by Tab Murphy, Bob Tzudiker & Noni White, directed by Kevin Lima & Chris Buck.

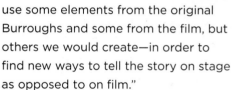

Both the music and the words for Broadway's *Tarzan* were written by world-renowned talents: Phil Collins (ABOVE), composer and lyricist; and David Henry Hwang (RIGHT), author of the musical's book.

Thomas Schumacher, president of Disney Theatrical Productions, produced the Broadway *Tarzan*.

"David has a great sense of how to adapt preexisting material and how to work in an ongoing collaborative process," summarizes Schumacher, which was a particular asset, "because we weren't asking for a script to be created from whole cloth. We would use some elements from the original Burroughs and some from the film, but others we would create—in order to find new ways to tell the story on stage as opposed to on film."

Schumacher had a clear-cut first choice for director, too—a man who had never before directed a Broadway musical, the renowned British-based stage designer Bob Crowley.

Crowley, of course, had been widely acknowledged for years as perhaps the theater's most outstanding creator of stage sets and costumes. In England, he has created dozens of productions for the nation's top performing arts institutions—the National Theater, Royal Shakespeare Company, Royal Opera, and Royal Ballet—as well as for the best of England's smaller contemporary companies, including the famed Donmar Warehouse and the Almeida Theater. For his work on the Broadway stage, Crowley has been nominated for ten Tony Awards, winning that top prize for *Carousel, The History Boys*, and *Elton John and Tim Rice's Aida*. He also designed *Mary Poppins*, Disney's co-production with legendary theatrical producer Cameron Mackintosh, first in London, then in New York City.

"Bob Crowley," says Schumacher, "is one of the most creative individuals working in theater today. He is a man of infinite vision, and he's been attached to this project since the beginning."

Crowley has very specific memories of beginning his work on *Tarzan*. "When the call first came," he remembers, "I think I just stared at the phone for five minutes, I was that surprised. I

Director and designer Bob Crowley (LEFT) confers with his producer.

mean, I remember seeing the animated film *Tarzan* in 1999 with Naomi Donne, our makeup designer, when both of us were working on *Elton John and Tim Rice's Aida,* and I loved every minute of it. I adored it. But I remember standing up as the credits were rolling and turning to Naomi and saying 'Well, this is one animated film that they'll never turn into a stage show.'"

In fact, the original idea was not to create a live-action *Tarzan* in the usual sense of a stage musical, but to produce it in some kind of large traveling structure, like a touring circus. And so Bob Crowley's early work on the production focused more on the way the tale would be told than what the tale itself would be, as the show seemed to get larger and larger the more people talked about it, until it seemed to be spiraling out of control—and out of scale.

"At one point we were considering two buildings," recalls Crowley, "we were going to hopscotch these buildings across the country and one would be under construction while we were performing in the other. The show was getting epic, and I think we began to get very tense that all our energies were going into where we were performing and not about what we were performing."

It became clear to Schumacher, at least, that they were on the wrong conceptual path, that the way into the heart of *Tarzan* was not to make it bigger

and more complex, but to move toward something much smaller. "So I sat down with Bob and said we should think about this as an intimate story, a domestic story, if you will, that happens in an intimate space," the producer remembers. "So we did various versions of what would be intimate space. Ultimately it just seemed that the story would play best, given all the options, in a proscenium theater.

"The idea of telling the story of *Tarzan* started as spectacle and was gradually simplified to a vehicle for the story we wanted to tell, and that's the personal story of Tarzan's coming of age. It's a story about family and it's a love story."

Some of the visual elements of the production did not change in the conceptual downsizing. "First of all," says director/designer Crowley, "the jungle would be completely abstract. There would be no literal vines on stage, although a lot would go on in the air. There would be a shipwreck event at the beginning, and that would be done with the Japanese-like simplicity of painted silk. Nothing would

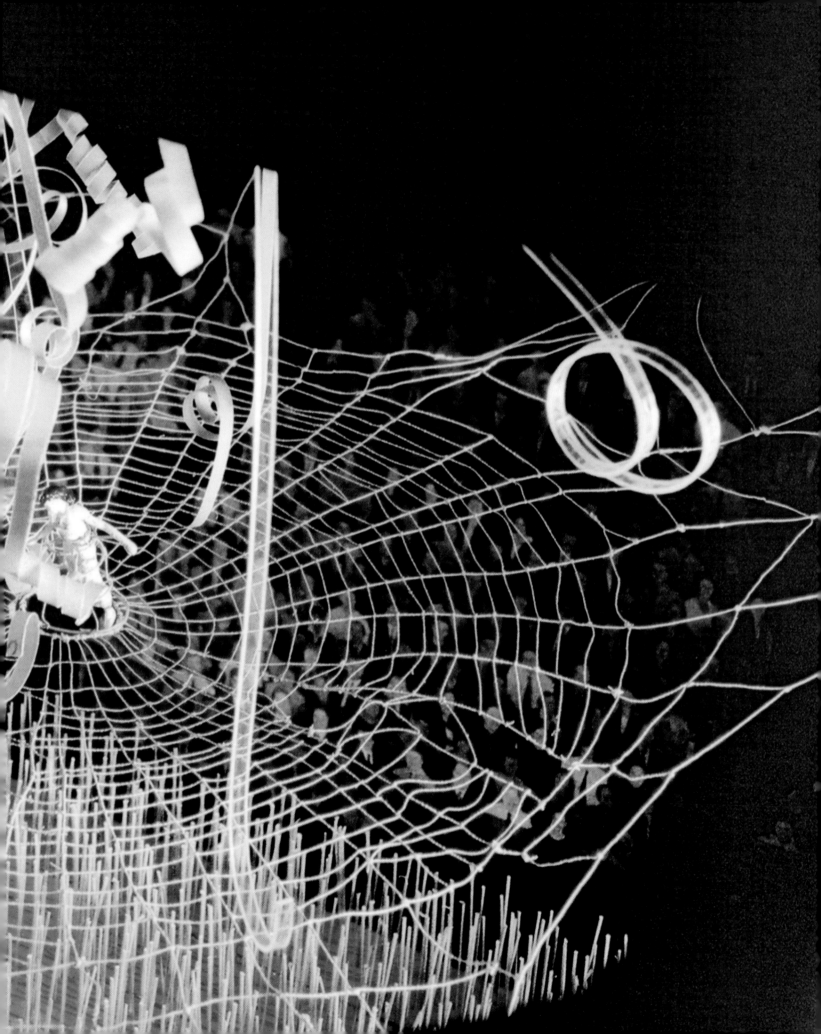

One of the central issues of the Tarzan design is the relationship between the physical world and the world of the imagination. This page offers one of Crowley's ideas for the shipwreck. OPPOSITE: The actors worked hard to invent a movement vocabulary for the show. INSET: A drawing of the "surfboarding" animated Tarzan of Disney's film.

look 'natural.' The reality would be highly theatrical rather than literal. Doing the show in a proscenium forced me into new solutions to things. And slightly wittier solutions to things, I think, that put the emphasis back on the performer."

Because the set is abstract, says Crowley, it would be just as suitable to other plays as it is to *Tarzan.* "You could do *As You Like It* on this set," he says, "or *A Midsummer Night's Dream.* That's not anything I intended, but I have noticed that it's happened before with abstract sets."

With Tarzan, of course, came the additional "issue" of flying—or the "problem" or "challenge" of flying, depending on how one chooses to see it. Since the very first film, audiences have thrilled to Tarzan swinging through the jungle on vines, and in fact a very old joke asks: What were Tarzan's last words? Answer: Who greased the grapev-i-i-i-i-i-i-ne?— spoken with one's voice trailing off into silence.

"We had to solve the flying problem," says Schumacher, "but we had to solve the movement question in general: how would Tarzan and the apes move on the floor? Would there be choreography? You don't really need dance numbers per se given that most of the characters in the show are apes. But what would the movement be?

"Around the same time, I had lunch with the animator Glen Keane. Glen animated the Beast in *Beauty and the Beast,* Aladdin in *Aladdin*, and Ariel in *The Little Mermaid*. Together we worked on *Pocahontas* and *Tarzan*. At one point, Glen, who was living in Paris, had this idea that he called over in the middle of the night: he had been watching his son, Max, skateboarding in a plaza. He got the idea, what if Tarzan moved like that in the trees, like he was skateboarding or surfing? There are only three or four minutes of that vine-surfing footage in the movie, but people remember it.

"So when I was talking to Glen about putting *Tarzan* on stage, I told him there was a big debate about how Tarzan would move and what we would do, because, I said, I can't simulate the vine-surfing. Now, Glen claims that this is my idea and I claim that it was Glen's idea, but somehow in the conversation he said you need another metaphor. Where surfing was the thing to do in the movie, you need something else for the stage version. Then one or the other of us said 'Rock climbing!'

"I immediately had an image in my head that became very clear. What if Tarzan's loincloth is actually a harness, with the carabiner that held him onto the rope totally exposed. Bob Crowley, who had actually seen an Icelandic production of *Romeo and Juliet* in which Romeo

MERLE DANDRIDGE

was on a bungee cord for the balcony scene, essentially had a similar idea at the same time. Because the exposed apparatus of the aerial work was part of the central metaphor of the show: that this is a theatrical reality, a universe different from nature but representing nature. So the movement became a combination of rock climbing and bungee jumping, and it also became part of the entire language of the production.

To choreograph, the team selected Australian contemporary ballet star Meryl Tankard. After having trained in her native country, Tankard became the muse of avant-garde German choreographer Pina Bausch. Schumacher had first met Tankard in 1984, when she was performing for Bausch at the Olympics Arts Festival, for which Schumacher had been instrumental in selecting the program.

Meanwhile, back in Australia, Tankard had also explored aerial ballet, creating a full-length ballet called *Furioso* in which various combinations of dancers performed on—and with—bungee chords. She had also choreographed an Andrew Lloyd Webber musical in London

The invention of an original movement vocabulary for Tarzan was assigned to Australian choreographer Meryl Tankard (LEFT) and Argentinean theater director Pichón Baldinu (BELOW), who has makes extensive use of aerial techniques in his work.

cast suspended from the ceiling of the theater for most of the show.

"Pichón who immediately understood the idea of exposing the technique," says Schumacher, "of letting the audience see the harnesses and the ropes. Because the show is not *about* swinging. It's not *about* flying. That's just a staging technique, like tap dancing. It's a tool used to tell a story and to be part of that story. And Pichón knew how to deliver that."

Now, virtually all original musicals go through a period of workshops. The writer, the composer, the director,

called *Beautiful Game,* which featured a danced soccer match that had impressed both Schumacher and Crowley. She had also dreamed up the *Deep Sea Dreaming* sequence which re-imagined the entire stadium as an aquarium populated by (flying) ocean creatures, for the opening of the Olympics in Sydney.

As for the actual *Tarzan* flying, the Disney team turned to Pichón Baldinu, a cutting-edge South American impresario who started his first experimental theater company when he was still a student in Buenos Aires. In 1993, he co-founded De La Guarda, a company dedicated to expanding the accepted limits of the stage. Baldinu and his company achieved worldwide recognition when they toured with *Villa Villa*, a totally original, freewheeling piece that was performed with the

JOSH STRICKLAND

JENN GAMBATESE

and the producer work their way to a solid first act or outline, assemble an appropriate group of singers, and semi-perform the piece as a work-in-progress. Such workshops are the first step in moving the show off the script page and onto its feet, and *Tarzan* was no exception.

Unlike most shows, however, *Tarzan* also had flying workshops, the first of which was held in Buenos Aires, where the creative team assembled for two weeks in 2005 to experiment with flying and the realities of gravity—not to mention the logistics of creating a nontraditional set.

"When we went down to Argentina," remembers Schumacher, "David had written the show. Phil had composed the music. But we were not yet committed to doing the show. We went to Argentina and tried to stage half a dozen major moments, the big set pieces. We needed to see how we could fly actors coming out of a wall covered with vines, how we could get them up over the audience. So we built a rig in an abandoned theater and spent two weeks learning how to

fly. We committed to doing the show because Pichón was able to demonstrate to us what we could do."

Back from Buenos Aires, Bob Crowley was able to complete the design for the set. But even before rehearsals started, there was one more workshop, for which the metal framework of the set was constructed on one of the stages at the Performing Arts Center of the State University of New York in Purchase, about 25 miles north of New York City. Here the cast, some of whom had appeared in De La Guarda in Manhattan, and all of whom had auditioned, at least in part, in midair, would begin to familiarize themselves with the environment they would inhabit and the theatrical language in which they would express themselves as members of the *Tarzan* cast.

The next step, of course, would be rehearsals. But where could a show like this rehearse? Normally musicals rehearse in rehearsal halls, of which there are several in Manhattan, the newest of them directly across 42nd Street from Disney's New Amsterdam

The first flying workshop took place in Buenos Aires, where the creative staff worked with actors from Pichón Baldinu's company to explore the possibilities of stage flight. This was followed by a second workshop at the State University of New York at Purchase.

31

Theater (home first of *The Lion King*, then of *Mary Poppins*). Shows rehearse for six or eight weeks and then move into their theaters for tech rehearsals and previews.

But *Tarzan* could not be rehearsed on a flat rehearsal-studio floor. The entire set would have to be built in order to safely prepare the actors for this production. But where could you get that kind of time in a big enough space in Manhattan? As it turns out, you can't. So the company was shuttled by bus, two days after Christmas 2005, to Steiner Studios in Brooklyn.

Steiner Studios opened in 2004 on 15 acres of what was once the famed Brooklyn Navy Yard (now decommissioned). There are vast open spaces surrounded by ancillary rooms that can be used for offices and support activities, and they were perfect for rehearsing *Tarzan*—a 120 x 135 foot soundstage (35 feet high to the grid) is more than big enough to hold the actual stage set for *Tarzan*, which was erected in the 162,000-square-foot Studio 2.

The space was also big enough to create what the production team referred to as "Rig Junior," a rough approximation of the actual set, where the actors could invent, develop, and practice their "flying" movements and could do so at the same time other scenes were rehearsing on the "Big Rig."

What space remained was divided into various work zones so that there was a music room, where music producer Paul Bogaev and music director Jim Abbott could work with the singers (or fight director Rick Sordelet could work out stage confrontations) as well as functioning "shops" for costumes, sets, and props. There was even

PHIL COLLINS

Sound Proof Enclosure

Walkway - Keep Clear

Storage / Rigging

Scaffolding

JOSH STRICKLAND, JENN GAMBATESE

Walkway - Ke

Main Rehearsal Area

ME RIGGER, YOU JANE

STEFAN RAULSTON
MARLYN ORTIZ

KIRK AENGENHEYSTER

a small area where the actors could rest, an orchestra "pit" (a platform with keyboard and drum kit), and an area dedicated entirely to the manufacture of the custom-made harnesses where Dany Conde labored day in and day out. As the actors rehearsed, the set and costumes were being assembled around them (which made fittings easier and concentration, perhaps, just a bit harder).

Upstairs were offices for production supervisor Clifford Schwartz and his stage management crew, and for company manager Randy Meyer and his staff. One room was set up as a music studio for the arrangers and orchestrators. There was a lunch room, a physical therapy room for kinked-up actors, and a classroom for Daniel Manche and Alex Rutherford, the two boys who would be playing Young Tarzan.

To start the first rehearsal, the entire company repaired to the music room (later christened the Jungle Room). Each member of the company stood and introduced him or herself to the others, from lead actors to prop and costume assistants. Everyone was introduced to the creative team—Bob Crowley, Meryl Tankard, Pichón Baldinu, David Henry Hwang, Phil Collins—by Thomas Schumacher. Then Bob Crowley did a short visual presentation of the set and costumes. After nearly five years in the planning stage, rehearsals had begun, and the entire company (one family of many worlds) was at the beginning one more time.

Stage 2 of the Steiner Studios at the old Brooklyn Navy Yard held the full set for *Tarzan*, a second experimental "jungle gym" dubbed Rig Junior by the crew, as well as costume and set construction shops and work areas for Ivo Coveney's special creatures and Dany Conde's custom-tailored harnesses.

CONFRONTING THE UNKNOWN

II

STEFAN RAULSTON

THE WORLD OF THE ACTION

THROUGHOUT THE LONG PROCESS that preceded the final concept for the staging of *Tarzan*®, one thing was always clear to director/designer Bob Crowley. The set would not be literal. "There was not going to be a leaf anywhere to be seen," said the Irish-born Crowley. And speaking of Ireland—or the jungles of the Congo—the set would be green.

In fact, the whole of Tarzan would be performed inside a kind of box. This "unit set" would anchor all the scenes of the show and tie them together both visually and thematically. Like the visible bungee cords the actors cavort on, the mechanics of the set would be visible, too.

The understructure of the set would be made of steel pipe. The rear wall of the box would be parallel to the back wall of the theater. Two side wings would extend at right angles from the back wall to the proscenium arch at the front of the stage. A giant gantry to operate the set pieces (as well as the actors) would be installed above the set and function out of view.

For safety's sake, the pipes of the main box would be embedded in inflated plastic (think of giant air mattresses). These soft walls would have free-form openings in them large enough for adult-sized apes to enter and exit (picture a swimming pool raft with cup holders blown up to enormous size). The clear plastic air bags would first be covered with green fabric; the fabric would then be festooned with thousands of "vines," actually just lengths of rope and fabric that represent vines—symbolically, poetically, and metaphorically.

Bob Crowley's model of the set of Tarzan at the Richard Rodgers Theater; schematic drawing for the complex openings in the rear wall; and cast members rehearsing above-the-ground entrances. The model shows both the final and preliminary notions for the tree house. NEXT PAGES: The cast rehearses the "Funky Monkey" in Brooklyn.

MARLYN ORTIZ

SEAN SAMUELS

ANASTACIA MCCLESKEY

JOHN ELLIOTT OYZON

The vines are actually made of two different materials. One is called Spanish web, which is a cloth-covered rope of the kind used by circus performers. This was made up especially for *Tarzan* in the show's signature green. The rest of the vines are made of Lycra, cut into long strips, and then pulled so tight that the fabric curls to the extent that it will not fully go back to flat. Each of the countless vines was attached to a green backcloth through a large grommet (like the metal rings a shoelace passes through) and was sewn on by hand.

There would be other sets, too, of course. The opening sequence of the show—which begins with a shipwreck—starts as a wash of inky, almost black, indigos, which gives way to an aqueous underwater moment before making a quick transition to a bright, almost white, beach. In fact, in the first ten minutes of *Tarzan,* there is no dialog whatsoever, just music and stagecraft. The idea was to let the stage tell the *Tarzan* story in the language of theater itself.

The *Tarzan* set, with its 50-foot, above-the-grid gantry that no one in the audience ever sees, weighs 88,000 pounds and includes 76,000 feet of vines, all of which were attached to the set by hand. Below: Associate scenic designer Brian Webb stringing vines with Bob Crowley.

As a designer, Bob Crowley is known for his manipulation of transitions between scenes, something he perfected in his many productions of Shakespeare. An Elizabethan play has far too many locations to create an entire realistic set for each one of them (although set designers in the 19th century tried it). Shakespeare's plays are far more practically (and poetically) designed by using a kind of visual shorthand—which is how they were mounted at The Globe—with small scenic pieces standing in for whole battlefields or castles.

Crowley likes to move his scenes fluidly from one to another, alternating that even flow with quick blackouts to entirely different locations. In a sense, his notion of stagecraft is highly informed by film. The scenes spill into one another smoothly, without stopping the action at all, like a film scene crossfading into the next. Furthermore, he often chooses points of view not usually associated with the stage (bird's-eye views of scenes, for example, with the back wall standing in for the ground and the audience seeming to see the action from a great height). It is part of Crowley's stage vocabulary to challenge audience assumptions about vantage points, about ways of seeing.

He is also known for the use of a great deal of fabric in his sets, a technique he has borrowed from theater traditions that go back centuries in some cultures. And Tarzan is no exception: the entire shipwreck takes place essentially on a painted silk drop. There is a silk waterfall in the production as well as silk grass and silk treetops. No one is supposed to "mistake" these lengths of fabric for the things they represent, yet everyone "gets it." Part of the fun of a Crowley set is that he creates sufficient reference points for the audience to fill in what's missing with their own imaginations.

Aiding and abetting Crowley in creating the settings for *Tarzan* were associate scenic designer Brian Webb, scenic design associate Rosalind Coombes, and assistant scenic designer Frank McCullough, who did a lot of their work at Steiner Studios before, during, and after rehearsals, and in the same room.

Lighting the set would be the great Broadway lighting designer Natasha Katz, one of the busiest artists in the business and one of the most popular with her peers. A four-time Tony Award® nominee, she won that honor for her lighting of *Elton John and Tim Rice's Aida.* (She's also done lighting for opera, for Las Vegas headliners, and for the American Museum of Natural History, for which she created the Big Bang light show at the planetarium).

Katz brings an extremely sensitive and evocative art of lighting to the creative table, which is backed by an encyclopedic technical knowledge of all the latest advances in lighting (of which there are many). She has likened the job of the theater lighting designer to the editor in film, in the sense that the lighting designer not only tells you where to look at any given moment, but underscores the mood of what you are seeing, the way you are meant to see it. In the case of *Tarzan* she was also responsible for adding much of the color to the production.

One thing that helped her was that the various materials and shades of the greens in the set do not all take light the same way, which she was able to exploit with an extensive use of ultraviolet light (like a disco's black light). "Some of the scenes," she says, "are completely lit with ultraviolet light." She notes that of the vines that "some go very very blue, others pop green, some go kind of gray, so you get this incredible texturing."

In fact, dealing with the vine box presented some unique challenges. "It took a couple of weeks to really start to understand the vocabulary of the green set," she says, even technically. "If you put red light on that set, for example, you don't get red. You get black. So there became a whole range of colors I couldn't use, or I had to figure out other ways of getting them."

In fact, a great deal of the color came to the lighting design fairly late in the process. "I think part of it was that we had to get comfortable with the way light worked on the set. And as we began to run the show, it became clear that every scene could not be green. I mean, even in the rain forest there are different times of the day—there are sunny days, there are sunsets, and we began adding those things."

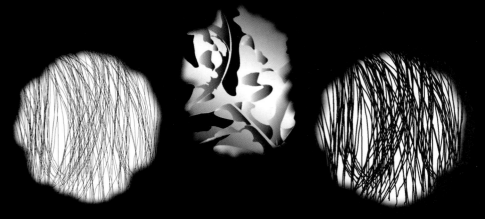

Tony -winning lighting designer Natasha Katz (ABOVE RIGHT) provided the illumination for *Tarzan,* both literally and, in some cases, figuratively. The circular black-and-white insets are not microscope views, but "gobos" that are placed in front of the lights to cast abstract foliage patterns on the set. Katz used 140 moving instruments and liberal doses of "black light" on the show.

CHESTER GREGORY II

KARA MADRID (FOREGROUND), CELINA CARVAJAL

Happily, Crowley, as set designer, provided several opportunities to move the palette away from green. The first scene of the second act, for example, "Trashin' the Camp" takes place in an intensely elaborate Victorian safari tent in tones of gold and red, tan and maroon. And Jane's entrance in the first act, her first encounter with the plant and animal life of Africa, offers a chance not only to fill the stage with carnival colors that approximate the bright costumes of the insects and exotic orchids but to direct the eye.

"Actually that happened quite late in the process. Now, we thought all along that the mechanics of seeing a giant spiderweb emerge from Jane's dress was going to be exciting, but it became apparent that we were giving it away too early. So, we needed to create a pleasant distraction. Since the whole scene has the personality of hallucination—because Jane is seeing things that nobody in the world has ever seen before— we went into colored light coming through the side walls and twirling on the back, and all the plants changing color all the time. So that when the spiderweb does appear, it's much more of a surprise."

And then there was the matter of the floor. "Well, the floor is heavily padded so the actors don't hurt themselves, and it takes light in a different way again from all the vines. Plus for many of the seats in the Rodgers, the audience is looking down on the stage floor. It becomes another whole canvas, and something has to happen on that floor that's as interesting as what goes onto the walls."

JENN GAMBATESE, JOSH STRICKLAND

One of the lighting effects in Tarzan that everyone seems to love is a kind of fluttering of light points that may be stars, or fireflies, or something else entirely. Certainly they are abstract, in a way that is different, for example, from the stars in Katz's design for the *Elton John and Tim Rice's Aida* light plot, where the stars look far more naturalistic.

"Well, that comes out of the collaboration with Bob Crowley," says Katz, whose team included associate lighting designer Yael Lubetzky and assistant lighting designer Aaron Spivey, among others. "We see that the first time in the show when the infant Tarzan turns into the boy playing Young Tarzan, and in the script, David Hwang wrote 'In the swirl of stars, years pass. A vocal shimmer echoes through the jungle.'

"We talked about it for weeks and months with this very idea that we didn't want it to look like anything we'd ever seen before. And I sort of fell upon these little points of light pulsing on the vines. And we see them again in the show, at the transformative moments of Tarzan's life. They become the signal that something important and magical is happening. So in that sense the light is actually trying to help tell the story. And that's what you always want. You want all the elements of a show to work together to tell the story."

Sometimes, happily, there are accidents that wind up improving the show. "You hear that all the time in the theater," Katz says. And *Tarzan* is no exception. "In the scene where Tarzan is learning how to be a man by watching the magic lantern show that Jane has set up for him," Katz remembers of the "Strangers Like Me" sequence, "well, those slides start out being projected onto a sheet that Jane has hung out to dry. And that's where the slide show was all supposed to happen.

"But one night the projector slipped and the slides wound up on the vine walls, which made them much bigger and kind of more interesting because they had such odd scale and texture. And everyone went, 'Oh, we love that.' So we kept it in, and that's what the audience sees now. It works because it explodes what Tarzan is seeing with his eyes to the magnitude of what he's experiencing in his head, where it was much bigger because, like Jane seeing the jungle flowers for the first time, this was the first time Tarzan was seeing anything like this in his life."

The final light plot of the production includes effects both designed and "found." Katz invented the shimmering abstract stars that appear in different guises throughout the show; the projection of the magic lantern slide show that Jane offers *Tarzan* during "Strangers Like Me" began as a fortuitous error when the projector was knocked out of focus during a rehearsal.

JOSH STRICKLAND

THE WORLD OF THE ACTORS

Bob Crowley's extraordinary design sketches for the apes capture the sense of movement he was after as the show's director. The costumes, made of thin strips of Lycra, contribute a theatricality that includes both human and gorilla characteristics.

THE ONSTAGE REALITY of *Tarzan,* from its inception, was that most of the actors in the show would be portraying apes. But how would those apes be realized? The first *Tarzan* film in 1918 (and many films afterward) employed extras in unconvincing ape suits that looked like moth-ravaged Halloween costumes. Characteristically, Bob Crowley wanted to create apes for this production that had a purely theatrical reality, one that made no attempt to disguise the athletic Broadway dancers whose job it is to portray the primate tribe in which Tarzan grows up and learns the ways of the world.

To that end, Crowley as designer, working closely with Crowley as director, envisaged costumes that were drawn from nature but that did not attempt to hide the actors wearing them. The apes of this *Tarzan* production would occupy an entirely theatrical universe. They would not "be" apes, they would represent apes metaphorically.

The mechanics of flying meant that the costumes, however hairy, would also have to be light and flexible to allow the actors the maximum range of movement. With the extra demands of flying in the show, the actors didn't need to be burdened with heavy costumes.

Having made his sketches, Crowley turned to "Special Creatures" wrangler Ivo Coveney.

Coveney, working with his wife Kay, a costume fabricator, presented Crowley with a selection of possible treatments for the texture of the ensemble's ape costumes. "Bob said, 'Have a try with different types of fur,'" Coveney remembers, "'but not fur. I want to give the impression of fur, but I don't want fur.'"

PRIMATE SURVIVOR

The chimpanzee that played Cheetah in the Johnny Weissmuller Tarzan movies (and who appeared in the 1967 film Dr. Dolittle *with Rex Harrison) was born in 1932 and currently lives in Palm Springs with the nephew of his original trainer. Cheeta has been declared by the* Guinness Book of World Records *to be the oldest living chimp ever documented.*

ANDY PELLICK

"So we had ripped silk and bits of cord and rags stitched on. And then we tried Lycra, cut very thin and pulled as tight as you can get it so it stays in a little tube, like long, hollow pasta. And then we stitched that on. We went to Bob with ten or twelve different samples, and he immediately loved the way the Lycra moved." The base for the Lycra tubing (an application almost identical to the set itself, also developed with the help of the Coveneys) is sewn onto the same lightweight perforated nylon used in the United States on professional football jerseys. That would offer all the stretch of a dance costume and be as light as possible.

The evolution of the ensemble costumes continued. Coveney came up with half a dozen or more possible ape shapes that he would realize with prosthetics to give the actors' bodies more of the silhouette of their less-evolved cousins. In Buenos Aires, working with Pichón Baldinu and his company, the design team even considered ape heads for the actors. But, says Coveney, "they always wound up looking like helmets."

As the development of the costumes continued, Crowley decided, they worked better conceptually, as well as practically, if the actors looked more like humans than apes. The attempt was made not to engage the audience with how authentically the costumes could mimic wild African fauna, but to engage the imagination of the audience in the simultaneous actor/role dichotomy, much as a performer in a mask might be said to have both his or her own identity and that of the character represented by the mask. The costumes are the cue the audience needs to let loose its imagination, to engage the suspension of disbelief, to accept those actors as jungle creatures.

CHESTER GREGORY II

48

ANDY PELLICK, JOHN ELLIOTT OYZON

During the flying workshop in Purchase, New York, the costume design team (which included associate costume designer Mary Peterson and assistant costume designer Daryl Stone) came up with the idea of slitting the lower part of the costume, the "leggings" of Crowley's drawings to allow more of the actors to show through the Lycra costumes. Sleeves got shorter, so did the "hair" itself in some cases.

All through the rehearsal and into the preview process, the costumes were simplified (as were the makeup and the wigs). In many areas, the preview period became one of subtraction rather than addition, of taking things away that obscured the actors or distracted from telling the story of a young man finding his true identity by finding his true love.

"When you pick up the costume," says Shuler Hensley, the production's original Kerchak, "it feels heavy. But when you put it on, it doesn't feel like you're wearing something cumbersome, because the weight is distributed around your body. My costume gives me a sense of vastness, but I don't feel like I'm struggling." (Of course, the Kerchak costume is nothing compared to the full-body rig Shuler wore as Frankenstein's monster in *Van Helsing* with Hugh Jackman. Getting into costume and makeup for that film took six-and-a-half hours. It only takes 45 minutes to turn Hensley into Kerchak.)

SHULER HENSLEY AND PEGGY KURZ (ASSISTANT WARDROBE SUPERVISOR)

On the actors, the costumes must work both while moving and at rest. The big picture on this page shows the "Jungle Funk" number in performance. Inserts include a company member at rehearsal, Terk in "Who Better Than Me?" and Kerchak having a costume fitting.

"THE COSTUMES ARE DESIGNED TO SHOW OFF THE ACTORS' BODIES, TO MAKE THE ACTORS APPEAR AS APES AND HUMANS AT THE SAME TIME. THEY AREN'T MEANT TO IMITATE NATURE. THEIR REALITY IS STRICTLY THEATRICAL, BUT BASED IN NATURE." —*TARZAN* DIRECTOR BOB CROWLEY

DWAYNE CLARK, ANDY PELLICK, MARCUS BELLAMY, STEFAN RAULSTON

HAIR AND MAKEUP

DIRECTOR BOB CROWLEY is credited by virtually everyone who worked on *Tarzan* (and by those who have worked with him before) as being absolutely at home in the collaborative process of making theater. He is not a dictator. He wants the people around him to contribute their best ideas.

Makeup designer Naomi Donne has worked with Crowley on numerous shows in New York and London—including Shakespeare's *Twelfth Night* at Lincoln Center, *Elton John and Tim Rice's Aida* on Broadway, and *Mary Poppins*—and knows how he works. "Well, he showed me the drawings, and I noticed that the apes' bodies has little squiggles all over them. But Bob didn't quite know what they were meant to be. He put them there as an intuitive gesture. It was up to me to figure out how to design a makeup plan that would work for the actors and the production.

"So I went back to all of his original research material, the same visual library he consulted when he designed the costumes. Lots of pictures of apes and gorillas. And it was up to me to translate that into a makeup scheme.

"Now, some makeup artists can make drawings of what they want to see on an actor's face," Donne says, "but I have to work on faces, so that's what I did.

"I grabbed one poor actor and painted his whole face with a gorillalike mask of makeup, something like the actors wore in *Cats*. I knew it was way too much, but I had to start somewhere. And in the course of working on the show, the makeup became less and less elaborate—because at the end of the day you want to preserve the actors' dignity and the eccentricities of their faces. We didn't want to hide them. Eventually their face makeup became just a single line, essentially."

Donne reduced the body markings Crowley had painted in his original sketches to "some flashes of color," she says, "as if the apes had just splashed themselves in color from the jungle."

The biggest challenge of the makeup plan, Donne says, was not aesthetic, but technical. "I had to come up with a formula that would allow the makeup to stay on the actors'

FUN FACTS: Five pounds of hairpins are used in every show to hold wigs in place. The cast uses two quarts a day of makeup remover.

In the makeup room, hair designer David Brian Brown helps Tarzan (Josh Strickland) with his dreads. OPPOSITE: Brown with makeup designer Naomi Donne. Donne used stencils to aid in the application of "flower" makeup for the dancers' faces.

faces and bodies but keep it from coming off on the set. It's one thing to wash a costume that has makeup on it," she says. "It's another to ruin the scenery."

Donne worked closely with hair designer David Brian Brown. It's almost a given of a musical that all the actors wear wigs, because the wigs hide their microphones and facilitate quick changes. In *Tarzan* only Professor Porter and Clayton appear on stage in their own hair. Professor Porter's microphone is threaded into the bushy sideburns that actor Tim Jerome grew for the part.

The wigs in *Tarzan* are made from human hair and were built in London to Brown's specifications. The human characters have fairly naturalistic wigs, including the dreadlocks that both the adult and the young Tarzans wear. This style is a carryover from the film but makes perfect sense: this is what hair would look like if it had grown for twenty years without being combed. And Jane has two wigs, one with her hair styled up, the other with it let down.

The ape wigs are a different story. Not only are they styled in a modified punk cut to capture the feel of Crowley's original costume sketches, but they have strips of Lycra sewn into them to match the feeling of fur from their costumes. Each costume and, therefore, each wig has several different colors of Lycra in addition to hair.

"We start with three basic hair colors," says Brown, "and then each wig has five or six colors of Lycra."

There are two basic versions of the ape wig—a male version, cut short at the sides and left spiky, and a female version, which has twisted hair in the front that approximates a row of braiding and somehow manages to invoke the elaborate hairstyles of native African women.

"I tried to do with the wigs what Bob was trying to do with the design of the show across the board," says Brown. "We kept asking ourselves, 'How do we make these creatures metaphoric and theatrical as opposed to imitating apes?' Kerchak has a bit of a built-up forehead and Kala has a little cage under the back of her hair for some height and to push the profile a little, but other than that, we weren't trying to reproduce what a gorilla looks like. What you see is just actor and hair…and Lycra, of course."

MARCUS BELLAMY

53

IT'S NOT ENOUGH, of course, for an ape in *Tarzan* to just look the part. He or she must act it. For the first step in their portrayal of members of the ape troop, Bob Crowley sent his ensemble off with some instructions right out of the Actors Studio.

"I told them very early on," says the director, "that I wanted them all to create their own family groups and to decide who was with who, and who's having babies with who and who isn't having babies with who and doing anything else with who. I said, 'You have to do that yourself. I'm not going to tell you. You decide, and come back with your own names.'

"Now I'm not going to quiz them on the personal history of each gorilla, but as an actor and a performer, when you come onstage you need to know exactly who you are, even if you're playing an ape. I mean, I'm blessed with a very beautiful cast, and they're all individuals. They're all very different in their personalities. And so the apes should be, too. And I don't know how much of this the audience sees, but it's up there onstage. The actors know."

The task of developing the apes' movement vocabulary fell to choreographer Meryl Tankard. She began to develop the way the apes would move in a workshop in Sydney, spending two-and-a-half weeks with a half-dozen acrobats, dancers, and aerialists, playing with ropes and harnesses. "That was about four years

ago," she says, making it around 2002, "and then things sort of closed down until suddenly they asked me to fly to Buenos Aires to work with Pichón. And when I got there I found he was just as surprised that the show was actually happening as I was."

Tankard started her research for the movement in *Tarzan* by watching gorillas, both on videotape and in person. "I remember that Bob Crowley and I went up to the Bronx Zoo to watch the gorillas, and, you know, they may be quite big, but their movements are very small. And I thought, 'Okay, how do I make a Broadway show out of that?'"

"So we cheated a little. I mean, if we were going to limit ourselves to gorilla movements, it was going to be a boring show for sure, so we went to watch the little monkeys, whose movements in proportion to their body size are much bigger than gorilla movements. So I borrowed some moves for the *Tarzan* apes from the monkeys.

DWAYNE CLARK

The entire cast began each rehearsal day with a 90-minute warm-up period of yoga and a South American form of martial arts called capoeira. In addition to their flying lessons, the ensemble members spent a good deal of time on floor work creating the movement language of the ape tribe.

MARLYN ORTIZ

CELINA CARVAJAL, JD AUBREY SMITH, MARCUS BELLAMY

GOING APE

KEVIN MASSEY

"One of the things we did, to get in shape and to get on the same page, was to start every rehearsal day with a 90-minute warm-up class. It was mostly yoga, but we added capoeira, a South American martial art, and it's great because the movements are very animal-inspired."

Tankard spent much of the early rehearsal time developing moves that all the apes would share, movements that would start with what she had seen at the zoo but that would develop organically into human gestures that embodied in their larger scale the essence of an authentic gorilla movement. Many of these movements were given names, like those in classical ballet, except these were taken from capoeira.

The backward somersaultlike move that both the young Tarzans and the adult Tarzan use throughout the production—a kind of back roll over one shoulder and a one-handed push-up back to standing—comes directly from capoeira (and is a cast favorite).

"And I had to teach them to stop moving like dancers, poor things," Tankard half laughs. "I mean, an ape's legs are short and its arms are long. Some of these beautiful dancers have these great long legs, and there I am saying, 'Keep your legs underneath you, don't extend—squat, squat, squat,' which is exactly opposite of all the training they've ever had."

One of the hardest things about learning the movements for Tarzan, of getting the movements actually into their bodies' memory, so that they didn't have to think about it, was that the movements, along with the flying, were making big demands on muscles they don't usually move. "I was sore all the time at the beginning," says one ensemble member. (Anticipating this painful discovery of new muscles, the production employed a full-time physical therapist to help the dancers work out their kinks.)

There were other consequences, too. An ongoing "joke" among the cast was that they were getting calluses on the tops of their hands from learning to walk on their knuckles.

RACHEL STERN

"And everyone participated," says Tankard, "the principals, the whole cast. It was all part of the process of making the show; it wasn't just for the dancers."

The heavily padded stage floor helped free the movements. "This way the actors can throw themselves around without hurting themselves at all, even on their knees," says Tankard, a dancer who has done her share of throwing herself around the stage in her career. "Part of the process was work, of course," she explains, "but part of it was like a big children's game."

There were ape skits to improvise and obstacle courses to master that would change each day. "We'd be climbing up and swinging down and going faster and faster," says one of the ensemble apes, "and Meryl would be calling out different moves that we would then have to incorporate while we made our way through the course." Work or game, the shared process helped the cast form a particularly close band of performers.

Between Steiner Studios in Brooklyn and the Richard Rodgers Theater, the cast spent one week rehearsing at the New 42nd Street Studios, which overlooks the New Amsterdam. (Here, "Jungle Funk," where the young apes intimidate Tarzan.)

THIS PAGE: Original ensemble member Stefan Raulston hoists one Young Tarzan (Alex Rutherford) in Brooklyn. OPPOSITE: Chester Gregory II works out his Terk moves at the New 42nd Street Studios, as does the other Young Tarzan (Daniel Manche).

"What was really interesting," says the choreographer, "was to see the changes in people from the auditions to the end of the rehearsal process. Some people—particularly those who had been in De La Guarda—were just confident all the way through. But some of the boldest of the dancers at the auditions became a bit more timid as we got into the flying. And then some of the more tentative actors just opened up."

Tankard worked with each of the principals individually to help them make the transition from actor to actor playing ape. Chester Gregory II, originating the role of Tarzan's best friend, says the tutorial allowed him "to really play around with the movement and come up with something that was organic for Terk." In fact, Tankard wanted all the apes to work with what was most natural to their own brand of movement—but to push themselves to new extremes.

All of the actors found the movement demands of the show both challenging and enlightening. In doing his research for Kerchak, Shuler Hensley spent some time watching real apes. "I took a lot of trips to the Bronx Zoo and to the Atlanta Zoo," he says, "not so I could mimic the apes move for move, but just to get an idea of when they move, what it means to move and the relationships they have with each other. You know, as actors, we think we have to be doing something all the time, but that's a fallacy. Some of the most meaningful moments are the moments of stillness and silence. Which then makes any movement that much more powerful. That's what I observed watching the real things. They move for a reason."

Merle Dandridge, playing Kala, found the biggest challenge was in a different kind of working process. "I think that Meryl and I work very differently, in that she works from the outside in and I work from the inside out. As an actress, everything I do onstage, every motion has to come from something in me. It comes

"I HAVE ALWAYS BE FASCINATED BY THE CONCEPT OF FERAL CHILDREN, OF CHILDREN RAISED OUTSIDE THE CONSTRAINTS OF HUMAN CIVILIZATION." —*TARZAN* DIRECTOR BOB CROWLEY

ALEX RUTHERFORD

Dysfunctional Ape Family Dynamics: Josh Strickland as an angry Tarzan confronts his adopted father, Kerchak (Shuler Hensley); Kerchak and Kala, Tarzan's adopted mother (Merle Dandridge) discuss their "different" son.

organically from what I'm feeling. So when I lose my baby in the prologue of the show, and I claw at myself—yes, that comes from the ape movement work, but it's because of my shock, my confusion at what has just happened. Once I can connect the feelings to the movements, the movements seem much more natural to me."

For Josh Strickland, what was most difficult was trying to process what Crowley, Tankard, and Baldinu wanted. "The first week of rehearsals was crazy," he remembers, "trying to learn everything and trying to do exactly what they wanted. By the second week, we could tell that they were very open to input from the cast, because we were creating these roles, and they were helping us create the movements with our bodies and what

was most natural to us. And that was great, being allowed to bring our own personalities into the process."

"You know," says Bob Crowley, "as a designer, part of my job is to have other people say no to me. I think up ideas, and either I say no to myself, or the director says no, or the producer says no, and I go away and come back with more ideas. As a director, I was trying to set up the opposite atmosphere. An atmosphere of 'yes,' where ideas were welcome and it would soon be clear to everyone which choices, which suggestions best told the story of the scene, of the play. You certainly get a richer result from that than just telling the actors what to do. If you hire creative actors, you want to give them the space in which to be the most creative they can be."

"IT WAS ONE OF THE AIMS OF THE PRODUCTION TO GIVE
ALL THE CHARACTERS A COMPLEX RANGE OF EMOTIONS."

TARZAN DIRECTOR BOB CROWLEY

WHEN GORILLAS FLY

THE "FLYING," of course—or the rock climbing, bungee jumping, and "pendulating," as Terk calls it in the show—are very much the center of the ape movements in *Tarzan,* and to perfect that aspect of the production, Tankard and the actors worked daily with Argentinian director/producer/ performer Pichón Baldinu, who loves being up in the air.

"What I like about suspending the actors," says Baldinu, "is that it introduces something new to theater. It changes the expectations by changing the physical world. It adds a whole dimension to the way the actors can

JOSH STRICKLAND

PICHÓN BALDINU, ANGELA PHILLIPS, WILL CARE

move in the space. What I love about flying itself is that it's a dream. It's a dream we all have. So flying in the theater is not just about changing the physical vocabulary of the art form, but of moving it past the literal to the unconscious.

"When someone like a ski jumper flies," Baldinu uses by way of example, "you think, 'He's flying,' but you also think, 'He's crazy; I would never do that.' My experience with flying in the theater is that people see it and they want to do it, too. It makes flying seem like the most natural thing in the world. It becomes a whole new element of inspiration."

The kind of flying that Baldinu has been experimenting with was just what the *Tarzan* creative team was proposing: exposed mechanics. In traditional stage flying, an actor is hauled up on a wire and moved through a fairly

How does Tarzan get to the top of the jungle? Practice! Josh Strickland and original ensemble members in early rehearsals at Steiner Studios (with Pichón Baldinu) and "the full monkey" in costume for a late run-through at the Richard Rodgers Theater.

VERONICA DeSOYZA

MICHAEL HOLLICK, RIKA OKAMOTO, HORACE V. ROGERS

narrow range of movement, and the audience agrees to pretend no one sees the wire. In fact, stage flying has changed very little since Mary Martin flew across the nursery in *Peter Pan*.

The *Tarzan* creative team had an entirely different notion: if anyone was going to hover above the ground in this show, the audience would see how it was done—whether the actor was playing an ape, a human, a leopard, a moth, or a flower. "Flying," like every other aspect of the show, would be symbolic: we know the actors are not flying, but we allow ourselves to experience them as flying by allowing theater to perform its transformative magic. Just as fully visible stagehands manipulate costumes and scenery in the Asian theatrical tradition, *Tarzan* would have frankly visible flying apparatus.

The safety of the actors is a high priority on the *Tarzan* set. Four professional climbers are part of the 50-person team that runs each performance. Pictured, FROM LEFT, ensemble member Rika Okamoto, climbers Paul Curran and Thorvald Jacobson with stage manager Frank Lombardi standing behind them, and Pichón Baldinu.

"What many people underestimate," says Bob Crowley, "is the power of the audience, of the audience's imagination. And that is really one of your greatest resources when you're working in theater. I mean, it's been going on since Shakespeare: you say you're on the fields of Agincourt or in Hamlet's castle, and the audience does the rest."

"The goal of the flying," says Baldinu, "is not virtuosity for its own sake. I'm not just interested in showing perfect form, like that of a gymnast. My point is to create emotion that is linked to the excitement of the experience, that is linked to our dreams, our imagination, to liberate the imagination.'"

Baldinu and Tankard shared certain fundamental ideas about developing the movement for the show. "Meryl approached the movements very much the same way I did," says Baldinu, "from real behavior in nature, but extended for the theater. We were hoping that the movement would seem organically related whether the actors

are on the ground or above it. We both like the reality of nature, and we both like to play."

But before you can play, you have to know the game. "The idea was to give everybody the tools to be in the air, to get used to the harnesses, to lose their fear. Because the first thing you need in flying, just as in life, is confidence. You have to feel that you won't crash, that if you jump in the air, the rope is going to hold you. We have to learn that by experience."

Part of the difficulty in choreographing above the floor "dance" numbers like "Jungle Funk"—or "The Funky Monkey," as the cast calls it— was the technical problem of keeping the climbing lines and bungee cords in order. "Sometimes I felt like I was knitting the numbers," Tankard jokes, "with that wire has to go under that wire, and that cord goes under and loops across."

"The difficulty of the show," says one of the swing performers, "was not teaching the movements to the cast. The difficulty was finding out what the set would accommodate." (Add to that the precise demands of computerizing all the flying in the show, and you get a taste of how difficult and tedious the tech rehearsals could get.)

New technology also aided the collaboration on the creative team. Phil Collins, for example, was particularly open to Tankard's suggestions for big dance numbers like "Jungle Funk," and Tankard is appreciative. "He is such a sweet guy," she says of Collins (a universal assessment in this company). "He brings such a gentle energy with him. And I'd be down there in Australia, and he'd be in Switzerland, and I'd say, 'Could we have a little change here, with nothing but drums?' And he would just sit down and work it out and e-mail me little snippets of drumming that I could get on my computer."

MARLYN ORTIZ, STEFAN RAULSTON

"ALMOST EVERY PRODUCTION DECISION WE MADE IN THE COURSE OF THE REHEARSAL WAS TO SIMPLIFY— THE SET, THE COSTUMES, THE SCRIPT. WE TRIED TO HONE EVERY ELEMENT SO THAT IT HELPED TO TELL THE STORY WE WANTED TO TELL." — *TARZAN* DIRECTOR BOB CROWLEY

MARCUS BELLAMY

Not all the flying the cast mastered wound up in the show. Jenn Gambetese, as Jane, for example, did all the physical workshops and a lot of aerial work. "I knew even at Steiner that a lot of my flying would get cut," she says, "but it was great to learn how to do it and to challenge myself. In the show, I don't fly a lot, but I do have to sing "For the First Time" while being lowered from the gantry, and that took some getting used to."

Shuler Hensley participated in the flying work, too, although Kerchak doesn't fly in the finished production. As the character developed, it seemed to the actor, the director, and the rest of the creative team that Kerchak was more Kerchak-like if he stayed on the ground. "Silverbacks don't swing between trees," says Hensley of his character, "they move trees."

For Chester Gregory II, the show's original Terk, the difficulty was overcoming a lifelong fear of heights. "At my first audition," he says, "I hung upside down and sang. I was petrified. And I wasn't used to it, so it hurt the next day—everything hurt."

For the "Trashin' the Camp" number that opens Act II, Gregory now enters on a zip line from the ceiling of the Richard Rodgers Theater, hanging upside down and singing, making his way onto the stage where he proceeds to scat-sing while dismantling the human's tent with the rest of his troop.

"Of course," he remembers, "Meryl wanted to make sure I moved like an ape the whole time. I'd be trying to slip in a little Michael Jackson stuff, and she'd be saying, 'Stay ape. Stay ape!'"

"In one sense," says Baldinu, "theater is about pretending. But with flying, there is no pretending. You don't have to pretend to be hanging upside down over the stage—you *are* hanging upside down over the stage. The biggest challenge of the flying is the physics of flying, just the pure gravity of it—and of keeping the actors safe.

"In Brooklyn, at the Steiner Studios, the real rehearsal space for me was Rig Junior, that second stage. It gave the cast a place to train, to fly, to understand what it means, how it feels in their bodies, to build up this new knowledge before applying it to the main stage, where the actors had to learn how to walk down the wall and move as if swimming underwater."

Among the other reasons for the daily yoga/flying/martial arts classes, in addition to warming the cast up for the day, was to bring a diverse group of people to a common vocabulary of movement—because the actors in the Tarzan cast have very different backgrounds. Some are primarily actors; some are basically trained as singers; others have classical dance training. A few have gymnastics in their backgrounds, one has been a Radio City Rockette. A handful actually had stage-flying experience before as members of the De La Guarda cast.

More jungle antics (FROM LEFT): Choreographer Meryl Tankard teaches Jane (Jenn Gambatese) to swing; Chester Gregory II flips while "Trashin' the Camp" with ensemble member Stefan Raulston; and Marcus Bellamy menaces as Sabor on the proscenium arch.

"With some of them, I thought, Will they ever be able to do this?" admits Baldinu, "but they tried and tried, and they wound up with the ability so internalized that they are making up new moves for themselves, trying new things. It's not just the audience that is liberated by the flying, it's the actors, too, and they can bring that freedom, that confidence, to all their work, not just to flying."

JENN GAMBATESE, JOSH STRICKLAND

"OUR TARZAN IS YOUNG. HE'S NOT YET
FULLY FORMED. HE DOESN'T KNOW
WHO HE IS." — *TARZAN* DIRECTOR BOB CROWLEY

JOSH STRICKLAND

TARZAN

"From the time we first started talking about the stage version, it was clear that neither of us wanted to do the cliché Tarzan®. We wanted to inject some youthful vigor and focus on the character at a point in his life where he's still a boy, but very much on the cusp of being a man," explains Bob Crowley.

"This Tarzan means to be a sort of feral innocence…obviously innocent of the human world. But because he is human, he has instincts inside him that he can't understand. He knows he's not an ape, yet he has no other reference, so he's conflicted.

"In our story, Tarzan is a young man, a person in late adolescence who comes into his own as a man after having felt incomplete inside his family. He can't do the things that apes do routinely, but he can do other things that are impossible for the gorillas. Everything that is natural to him is considered odd or peculiar, even dangerous."

When Tarzan meets Jane Porter (stuck in a gigantic spiderweb in this production), he is seeing a human female for the first time, much as Miranda gets her first look at a human male in Shakespeare's *The Tempest* and utters her famous lines, "How beauteous mankind is! O brave new world, that has such people in't!" For Tarzan, Jane is more than a lovely young woman, she is the key to his identity.

One of the things that draws Tarzan and Jane together is that they are both possessed of a large measure of innate curiosity. "I find it to be one of the most attractive characteristics a person can have," says Crowley. "In the arts particularly, if you don't have it, it's like missing a limb." It's their curiosity that makes their mutual discovery scene so winning."

The "Me Tarzan, You Jane" scene, which has been substantially re-imagined, extended, softened, and leavened with humor by Crowley and David Henry Hwang, is the scene where this curiosity and innocence are most in play. Tarzan, who begins this story very much more ape than man, meets Jane in the jungle and, as apes do, he begins to mimic her.

"What I really love is to hear the squeals of delight from the young people in the audience during that scene, from the kids who don't have any preconceptions as to what Tarzan should and shouldn't be like. When Tarzan starts to imitate Jane and starts doing her inflections and her accent, even the youngest ones are completely wrapped up in it. It's a game they know, and they completely get the special ape/human spin on it that we have going on."

Broadway newcomer Josh Strickland sings "For the First Time" with Jenn Gambatese as Jane at a preview performance; Katherine Marshall, from Tricorne costumes, helps fit Strickland for Tarzan's legendary loincloth.

The task of creating the role of Broadway's first singing Tarzan came to rest on the shoulders of Josh Strickland, age 22.

"There were several things about Josh that made him perfect for the role," says Crowley. "He's young, for one thing. He happens to be extremely natural and unaffected in himself, and he was totally innocent in that he had certainly had no experience creating a title role."

"Josh came in with no experience of performing on Broadway at all," remembers producer Thomas Schumacher. "Then he sang 'Everything That I Am,' and we just couldn't believe it. No one we had seen had come anywhere close. He nailed it. Phil was amazed."

"We loved him," remembers Crowley. "He had a great voice, but clearly he was not going to be meeting the preconceptions of people who think that Tarzan should look like Johnny Weissmuller."

The creative team came up with a creative solution. They would postpone their casting decision. They would send Strickland off to train and ask him to come back. He could be in the show, but not, perhaps, in the lead role.

"I thought they'd want me to bulk up," says the actor, "but that's not what they were interested in. I worked with a trainer for about three months, three times a week," he says of his physical regimen, "and a yoga teacher, also three times a week. The focus was not bodybuilding but getting in touch with my body, because it is such a physical role that you just have to make sure that your body doesn't give out on you. It was more like core strengthening and getting loose."

Tarzan is defined by his "two worlds," the ape world is best represented by the young hero's relationship with his adopted mother, Kala; the emerging human Tarzan finds himself in his attraction to the human Jane. (Josh Strickland; Merle Dandridge, Phil Collins, and Strickland; Jenn Gambatese and Strickland).

"Josh did an enormous amount of work to win this role," says Michele Steckler, creative affairs senior Vice President for Disney Theatrical Productions. "He proved to us beyond any doubt that he would do what he had to do to make it work."

Josh Strickland is an incredibly likeable individual who's been preparing for a career in show business all his life, while growing up in Charleston, South Carolina. He started singing in the choir at his church, took dance lessons, followed his dream. He wanted to play Tarzan on Broadway—if for no other reason than his admiration and close identification with Phil Collins.

"Our voices are different," says Strickland, "but he was always somebody I'd listen to. We both have such high singing voices, I could always sing Phil Collins's songs in the key they were written—which is rare when you sing in this register." The aspiring performer had even sung a Collins song, "Against All Odds," for an appearance on *Star Search*.

"We cast him in the show but didn't commit to having him play Tarzan. We told him he'd either play the part or be the understudy," recalls Thomas Schumacher. "If he wanted the role, he would have to

work for it. Because being cast as the leading man in a Broadway show is about more than having a great voice. Even if he could play it, did he have the tenacity, the fortitude for the rehearsal process and the long performance haul. Did he have the winning charm to pull it off? The charisma to help carry the whole cast through any difficult moments?"

"I had never studied acting at all," admits the young star, "so Bob and Tom and the others were my teachers."

"I remember saying to him," recalls Schumacher, "no matter what happens, no matter what goes wrong—and something will—do not step out of character when you are on that stage.'"

The advice proved useful during one preview, in the scene where Tarzan fights Sabor. Strickland wound up hanging from his harness upside down, tangled in the rig worn by the actor playing the leopard. He didn't panic. He just hung there in character until the problem was resolved.

In addition to his physical prowess, his naturalness, and his native curiosity, Strickland had a few biographical connections to the character of Tarzan to draw on, too. "Well," he says, "we are both only children and we were both adopted," something no one knew when he was hired, "although I was not adopted by gorillas, obviously," he concludes, just to keep the record straight.

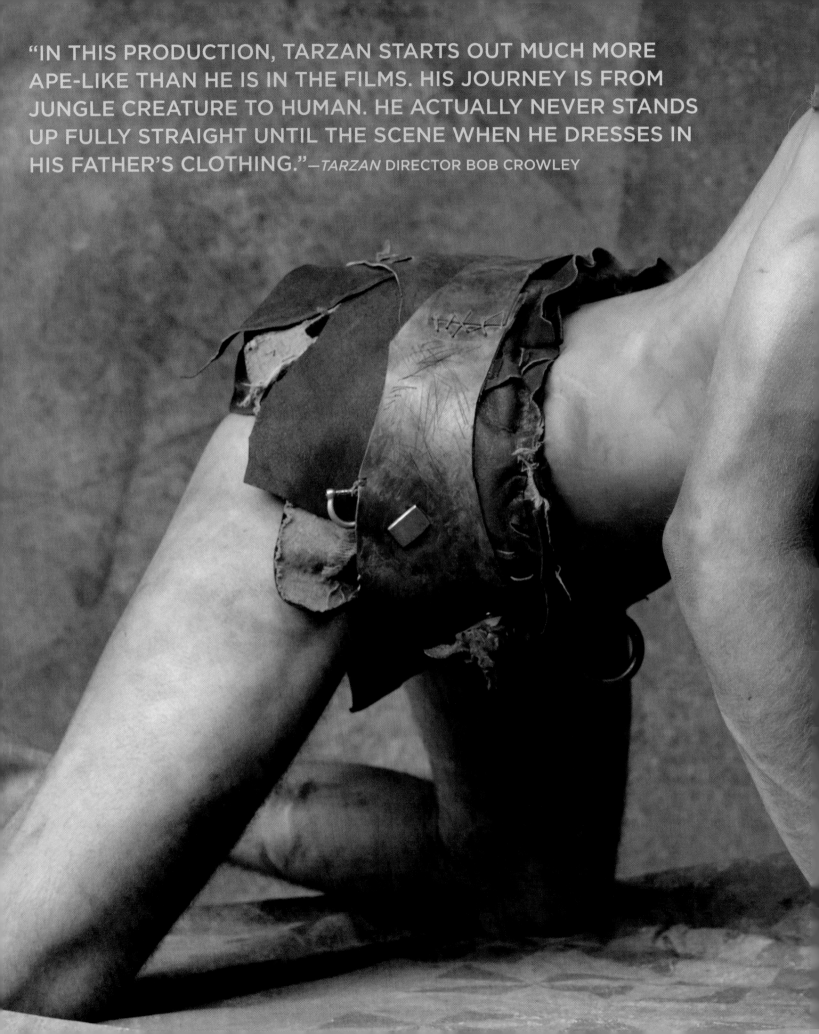

"IN THIS PRODUCTION, TARZAN STARTS OUT MUCH MORE APE-LIKE THAN HE IS IN THE FILMS. HIS JOURNEY IS FROM JUNGLE CREATURE TO HUMAN. HE ACTUALLY NEVER STANDS UP FULLY STRAIGHT UNTIL THE SCENE WHEN HE DRESSES IN HIS FATHER'S CLOTHING." —*TARZAN* DIRECTOR BOB CROWLEY

JOSH STRICKLAND

"HUMANS ARE SOCIAL CREATURES WHO NEED A SENSE OF BELONGING—TO A FAMILY, TO A COMMUNITY. WE HOPE THAT THIS SHOW WILL SPEAK TO ANYONE WHO HAS EVER FELT LIKE AN OUTSIDER."
—*TARZAN* DIRECTOR
BOB CROWLEY

ALEX RUTHERFORD

YOUNG TARZAN

ALEX RUTHERFORD, DANIEL MANCHE AND THEIR TEACHER, MARYANNE KELLER

Two boys alternate in the role of Young Tarzan. During rehearsals, they attended school together in a two-chair school room (ABOVE) and, of course, they rehearsed together every day (BELOW RIGHT).

THE MUSICAL BOOK of *Tarzan* could have begun anywhere in the story, but there was never any doubt in director Bob Crowley's mind that it would begin with Tarzan as a child. Not only is there precedent in the book and the animated film, but it's an appropriate decision for family entertainment. Kids identify with kids. And if you want to emphasize a character's essential innocence, there is hardly a better way to do it than to introduce him as a child.

Having a boy start the role, while it presents certain logistical problems, like coordinating their schooling and rehearsal schedules, dovetailed with one of Bob Crowley's particular curiosities. "I am absolutely fascinated by the idea of feral children," he says, "of children who grow up on their own, outside of society." In fact, he says, François Truffaut's *The Wild Child* (1970) is one of his favorite films. It's a notion that obviously appeals to others, too. *The Jungle Book*, based on Rudyard Kipling's tales of a boy raised by wolves in India, was the No. 1 box office film of 1967, the year of its initial release.

Crowley had held the image of a small boy on stage "touching your heart" right from the beginning of his work on the production. Largely because of this, he was happy to let go of the monumental traveling production as originally conceived for the intimacies of a proscenium theater as small as the Richard Rodgers. "I Need to Know," the lost boy's lament, could easily have been swallowed up in a huge amphitheater.

To create the role of Young Tarzan, the production hired two young actors to alternate performances. And although the two were quite different physically, onstage—in their dreadlock wigs—they appear almost interchangeable.

Like many child actors, the original Young Tarzans—Alex Rutherford and Daniel Manche—were quick studies, and both took immediately and fearlessly to the physical aspects of their role, Crowley, Meryl Tankard, and Pichón Baldinu all report. "I kept having to remind the boys that they shouldn't be doing things too well," says Tankard. "Remember, that your character is just learning how to do these things."

"The boys are extremely affecting," says their director, "and when they come out in the curtain call—after they've been absent from the action for an hour and a half—they get a very big burst of applause."

ALEX RUTHERFORD, DANIEL MANCHE, CHESTER GREGORY II

KALA & KERCHAK

IN DISNEY'S ANIMATED FILM, Tarzan's parents—Kala and Kerchak—are fairly straightforward, uncomplicated characters, more or less one dimensional: Kala is the epitome of nurturing motherhood; Kerchak is the grumpy, remote father figure. In the final stage version, they are both far more nuanced, and far more complete as characters, theatrical characters rather than cartoon characters.

Both roles have been significantly expanded. Kala still sings "You'll Be in My Heart," but Kerchak now has a solo, too, "No Other Way." And the pair of them have a new duet, "Sure as Sun Turns to Moon." Additionally, they have much more interaction with Tarzan and with each other and are much more integrated in the fabric of the story and the physical production.

As is the way with developing productions, some of this was planned, some of it was deemed necessary in the course of rehearsals, some may be credited to the unique gifts of particular actors hired for the jobs, in this case Shuler Hensley (Kerchak) and Merle Dandridge (Kala).

"Tom Schumacher said that during the making of the movie, they finally agreed that the less Kerchak said the better," reports book writer David Henry Hwang. "Kerchak was not a talker. He didn't explain things. But it's easier to do that in an animated film than it is onstage when you have a flesh-and-blood actor up there. So it was clear that Kerchak would have a bigger and more active role, and would be a more humanized character."

Kala, the good wife and tender mother of this ape family, plays a pivotal role in the arc of Tarzan's emotional development. Here, from left, Merle Dandridge confers with Kerchak (Shuler Hensley), tries out her prop ape baby, and in performance with "You'll Be in My Heart."

"For one thing," says Bob Crowley, "we were worried that a father dragging a seven-year-old child into the jungle, probably to die, would just seem ghoulish—very Brothers Grimm. If he is that heartless, then Kerchak would never get the audience's sympathy back, which he must have for the balance of the whole story. But Kerchak is a good leader and he's not such a bad father. He's definitely not heartless."

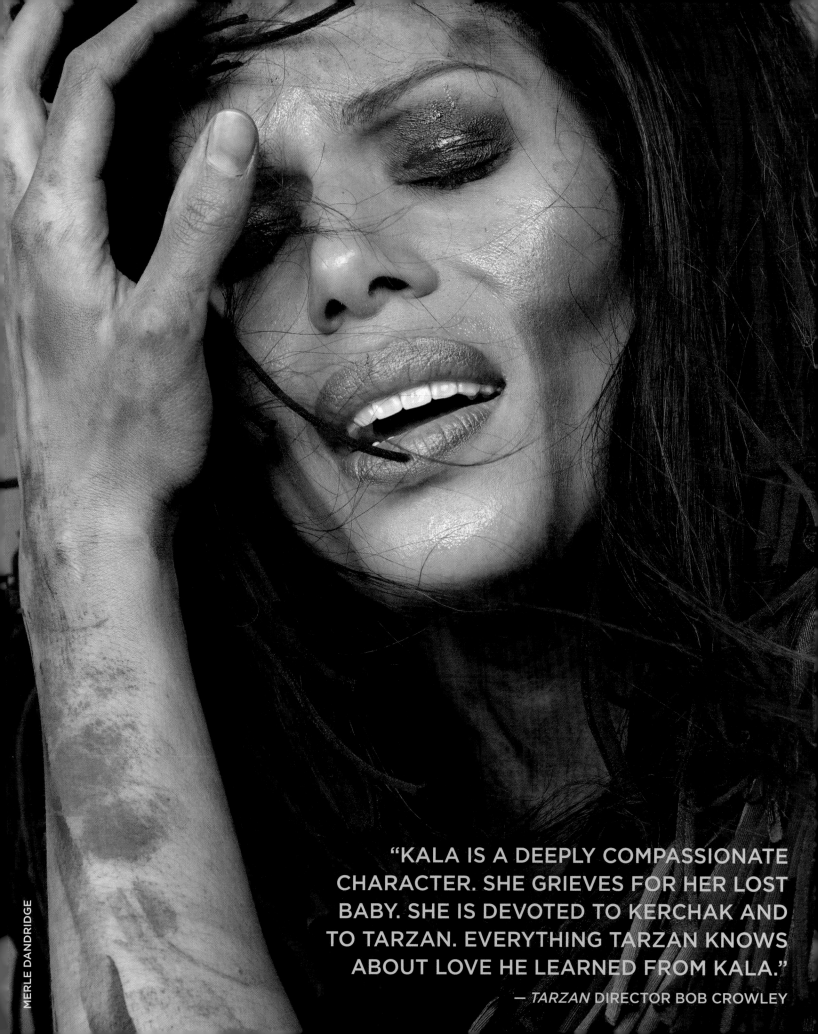

MERLE DANDRIDGE

"KALA IS A DEEPLY COMPASSIONATE CHARACTER. SHE GRIEVES FOR HER LOST BABY. SHE IS DEVOTED TO KERCHAK AND TO TARZAN. EVERYTHING TARZAN KNOWS ABOUT LOVE HE LEARNED FROM KALA."
— *TARZAN* DIRECTOR BOB CROWLEY

In the stage version of *Tarzan*, Kerchak not only sings, but he feels—deeply. As created by actor Shuler Hensley, Kerchak, like Kala, is motivated by love—for his tribe, his family, and the lost family of his childhood.

"I understood that there was plenty of story without developing the role of Kerchak," says Hensley, "but if you are shaping a story about a young man's journey from childhood, where he feels alienated, to adulthood, where he finds a place that he belongs, then the relationship with his father figure is vital. Both Tarzan and Jane are shaped by their relationships with their fathers."

"So," remembers Crowley, "we rewrote the scene so that Kerchak is actually instructing Young Tarzan in ways to keep safe. Shuler certainly has the power as an actor to be sympathetic, and obviously the parents in the audience understood that some decisions, however hard, have to be made. Because the first time we played the new scene in previews, there was a much bigger hand from the audience for Kerchak during the curtain call than there had ever been before."

If Kerchak was to be softened, Kala was going to be given a new edge. No more a mere doting foster mother to Tarzan, Kala would be given a ferocious side, too, right out of the original book by Edgar Rice Burroughs. She, too, could fight, particularly for her child, and she had to have enough substance to defy Kerchak.

Which led to yet another new scene, and song, that was inserted during the rehearsal process. "We had to ask ourselves," says composer Phil Collins, "if Kerchak is such a miserable bugger all the time, why would anyone want to marry him? Especially Kala, who is the good mother figure. At one point I wrote a song called 'Protect the Family,' which was a kind of marching in time. But a few weeks before rehearsals began someone brought the problem up again. And someone else said, 'We have to show why Kala is so committed to Kerchak.' And someone else brought up 'Do You Love Me?' from *Fiddler on the Roof.* And that led to 'Sure As Sun Turns to Moon,' which also recalls a song like 'I Remember It Well' from *Gigi*."

SHULER HENSLEY, MERLE DANDRIDGE

The remote father in Tarzan's adopted family, Kerchak (Shuler Hensley shown) is driven by a fierce and loving protectiveness for his tribe and for Kala; he refuses to engage young Tarzan emotionally because he honestly believes the boy is a danger to his blood family.

"It's the most theaterlike song he wrote," says Tarzan's music producer, Paul Bogaev, "I mean it's like Sondheim in a way. It has a kind of a rhythmic motor going on, and it is definitely a dialogue scene that's been set to music. It's one of my favorite things in the show."

The great advantage of originating a Broadway role is that the actor can leave his or her imprint on the character, not just in the way she or he plays it, but in the way the part comes to be written. "Halfway through the development process," remembers Tom Schumacher, "we were approaching Kala very much the way Glenn Close played her in the film—and as Cass Morgan played her in one of our workshops. Then Merle Dandridge came in, and she had this warrior mother thing down, which I loved."

"Well," says the mellow-voiced Dandridge, "what I didn't see in the movie was the beast in Kala, the animal. She's as tender as she's portrayed, but she's also got the other side, which I think most mothers do. And it's in the book. Burroughs says that no creature had ever been as fierce in their love as Kala was for Tarzan. That connected me to the animal side of Kala and gave me a lot of license."

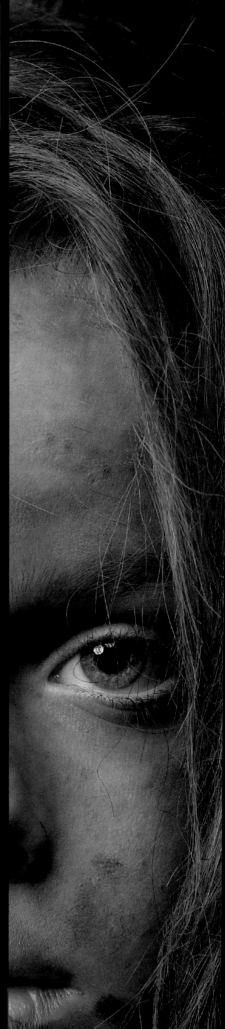

And the same is true of Shuler Hensley (who spent time observing both zoo animals and his own children for clues to Kerchak's behavior). "When Shuler Hensley came in to audition," remembers Thomas Schumacher, "he was totally not what we wanted for Kerchak. Then something unusual happened. He reinvented the role for us during the audition. He completely turned us around. Which is a tribute both to Shuler and to our casting director Bernie Telsey. He did such a beautiful job casting for us."

When Hensley (who won a Tony® for his portrayal of Jud Fry in the recent Trevor Nunn revival of *Oklahoma!)* signed onto *Tarzan,* there wasn't even a Kerchak song. Shortly after he agreed, however, Hensley would find out what it's like to have a song written specifically for his role and his voice. A large part of the rehearsal process for Shuler and Kerchak was softening the character so he didn't seem quite so remote, so mean, so relentlessly cranky.

"Kerchak isn't the villain of the piece," says Hensley. "Clayton is the villain. Kerchak may be dark, he may be a 'heavy,' but what interests me about those characters is the hidden redeeming qualities in them which enable everyone to relate to them. Kerchak can't just be a gruff, blowhard gorilla for two hours. Who would care about him?"

Crowley is enthusiastic about both of Tarzan's ape parents: "Both Merle and Shuler are both serious actors with glorious voices, which is really a blessing when you're producing a musical. Merle brought such physical and inner beauty and such intelligence to the role; Shuler contributed hugely to defining Kerchak. I'd say that working with them was a true collaboration between actors, director, and playwright. Because they've brought themselves to those characters, and those characters are now different as a result of casting those actors, and that's absolutely how it should be. You rewrite to an actor's strengths."

"BOTH KALA AND KERCHAK UNDERSTAND THAT BEING A GOOD PARENT MEANS MAKING DIFFICULT AND SOMETIMES PAINFUL DECISIONS." — *TARZAN* DIRECTOR BOB CROWLEY

ALEX RUTHERFORD, MERLE DANDRIDGE

"IF IT WEREN'T FOR TARZAN, TERK WOULD PROBABLY BE THE MISFIT OF THE TRIBE."
— *TARZAN* DIRECTOR BOB CROWLEY

TERK

DURING THE DEVELOPMENT of the script in its early days, reports David Henry Hwang, Tarzan's sidekick was reduced from a trio of apes to one, Terk. Wise-cracking, plain-speaking, and irreverent—like a Shakespearean fool—he's designed as a crowd-pleaser and he carries a good measure of the entertainment value of *Tarzan*.

Defining Terk and making his scenes with Tarzan work turned out to be tricky. "We got as many as three sets of revisions a week," remembers Chester Gregory II, the actor cast as Terk. In fact, of all the scenes in the show that were rewritten, Terk's Act I scene with Young Tarzan was, perhaps, rewritten the most. The thrust of the scene hasn't changed, but the specifics have.

Gregory's easy rapport with book writer David Hwang helped him in the process. "They gave me the liberty to improv a little bit," he remembers of the rehearsal process, "and David would know when I was just joking or when I actually thought we could make something work, or when something spur of the moment could be incorporated into the show. He was very flexible. He's a very lenient and kind man."

Actually, Hwang says, he is only lenient to a point. "I'm happy to listen to anybody," he says, smiling, "partly because that's my job and partly because I know I don't know everything. But once everyone agrees on a line, I want to hear the line as written and not something else."

And then there was the song. In both acts, Tarzan and Terk (in Act I, it's Young Tarzan, in Act II adult Tarzan) sing a version of the same song. In the original script, that song was called "I Believe in You," which, Phil Collins says, is one of the songs he wrote for the show that he likes the best. But in the second act, in particular, it just wasn't working. Then, during a rehearsal just before previews began, Chris Montan, president of Walt Disney Music, leaned over to music producer Paul Bogaev and said something to the effect that, "We need something more upbeat, more up-tempo here."

The collaborators huddled and agreed. Phil Collins went off and wrote a new song, "Who Better Than Me?" and, suddenly, a scene that just wasn't quite clicking was rocking. Partly because Chester Gregory II seemed to feel the new song much more completely.

"You know something is working," says Bob Crowley, "when it takes the actors absolutely no time to learn it and make it their own and bring it to performance level. And that's how it was with 'Who Better Than Me?'"

Terk, Tarzan's best friend (Chester Gregory II), offers his assistance in "Who Better Than Me?". TOP: Gregory surrounded by (FROM LEFT, associate director Jeff Lee, Bob Crowley, Tim Jerome, and Thomas Schumacher.

"TERK PROVIDES A GREAT DEAL OF THE FUN OF THE PRODUCTION. AUDIENCES LOVE HIM." — *TARZAN* DIRECTOR BOB CROWLEY

CHESTER GREGORY II

JANE

As conceived for this production, Jane (Jenn Gambatese pictured) is a well-educated young Englishwoman with very little experience in life. The audience meets Jane as she meets the jungle for the first time, its rich plant life played by members of the ensemble.

THE ARRIVAL OF JANE PORTER in Tarzan's world is the catalyst for his self-discovery and transformation. Not only is she the first member of his species that he's ever seen, but his growing love for her wakens feelings inside him that have confused him all his life.

"I think she's as innocent as he is," says Bob Crowley. "She's met men, but she's essentially a bookworm. She'd like to be in love, perhaps, but she has a father to tend to and no doubt a household to oversee since her mother died in addition to her own studies. And in her way, she's absolutely fearless."

"Well," says Jenn Gambatese, the actress cast as Tarzan's great love, "Jane has only known these jungle flowers before from books, and suddenly they're in front of her eyes, and she says they feel like friends. Which implies to me that maybe she didn't have a lot of friends back home with her father and her extremely unusual education. And that outsiderness is one of the connections between Jane and Tarzan.

"I am personally not nearly as fearless as Jane is," she continues. To find her character she had to do a little reverse acting work: "Usually you look into yourself to find the characters, but I had to look to Jane and to borrow her strength, not just for the character but for me, as an actress, to get through it all.

"Greg Gunter and Ken Cerniglia from Disney Theatrical brought me some dramaturgical material that helped a lot with the research," she says. "One was a book called 'How High Can You Climb?' It was stories of women explorers. That was inspiring, because I wonder if I have the guts to do something like that. Not naturally, but it sure seems worth it to me to try."

"She blew us away at her first audition," says director Bob Crowley, "because she had a delightful kind of curiosity and energy about her and that lovely, fresh gamine quality that I was looking for as well. And she's a little bit tomboyish, too, which is very endearing. Like an Italian movie actress from the '50s. Judi Dench has the same quality. She's feminine, but she's the kind of girl who wouldn't be afraid of frogs and snakes, and who would absolutely go off to Africa with her father."

"It is so overwhelming, starting a new Broadway show and originating a role," says Gambatese, "and your mind can just start, I call it ticker taping. It goes 'tch-ch-ch-ch-ch' a mile a minute. And I had to really say, 'Okay, but for Jane, this is not a big deal. For Jane, this isn't an accent, this is just the way she talks. For Jane, these are the perfect notes to be singing this song because that's what she's expressing.'

In fact, the whole audition process for a Broadway show is something of an adventure." You walk into a big room," she explains, "and there's a table at one

"TARZAN AND JANE SHARE A
REAL CURIOSITY ABOUT LIFE."
— *TARZAN* DIRECTOR BOB CROWLEY

As Disney fans will recognize, the line "Man in the forest," comes from the animated classic, Bambi. It is a signal of danger used by the forest creatures when a human enters their domain. In the early days of the Disney Studio, Walt Disney made a habit of appearing unannounced in the Animation Building, which was unsettling to the animators (for whom "working" sometimes meant sitting and staring at their boards, smoking their pipes, or chatting among themselves). The animators started using "Man in the forest" as a code for "Walt is in the Animation Building." That way, every time the Studio founder wanted to see how the next project was coming along, his animators were busily engaged in sketching.

JOSH STRICKLAND, JENN GAMBATESE

Like Tarzan, Jane, too, is torn between two worlds, the comfortable known world of her father, the good-hearted Professor Porter, and the complex, dangerous, and disorderly world of her own heart, which longs for adventure (and Tarzan).

JENN GAMBATESE

end, and behind the table is a whole panel of people, not the least of whom is Phil Collins. And, of course, the song they give me to audition with is 'Waiting for this Moment,' which happens to be almost all in Latin, all the botanical plant names.

"So I muddled my way through it, and when I finished, I said, 'I can't believe I just bit in front of Phil Collins.' It was supposed to be an interior monologue, but out it came."

"Jenn was an example of exactly how to arrive at an audition," remembers Thomas Schumacher. "She came in wearing the perfect dress, perfect shoes, perfect hair, and did a reading, and we all fell in love. We just said she is the right shape, she is the right size, everything is about her is right."

"So, playing devil's advocate, and because I really didn't know, I said, 'Is this music inside of her?' Because she is a legit Broadway person, not a rock/pop singer. But Phil knew. He said, 'Oh, I'll show you,' and he had her back for a private session."

"So back I came," says Gambatese, "and I was walking into the rehearsal hall for a private tutorial with Phil Collins, and I thought, 'If this process doesn't go any further than this for me, it will be one of the highlights of my career.'"

As for Jane, says Jenn, "She's a joy to inhabit. She's smart, she's funny, and she marches to the beat of her own drummer—and I don't mean Phil Collins.

"I worked a lot with Bob and with Paul Bogaev, particularly with the songs. I mean, Jane enters the action of the play for the first time singing the Latin names of plants. So aside from actually learning how to pronounce them, I had to find out what these flowers mean to her. And that was part of the key to her character and to her relationship with Tarzan."

Actually, Gambatese auditioned for *Tarzan* once before. "It was back in 2002, when they were casting for the first workshop. There was a tiny jungle gym set up. Bob Crowley was there, of course, and I thought I gave a good audition. I remember Bob came over and gave me some notes, and I was like, 'What a great guy! I would really love to work with him. And I feel like I can really do that part.' But they wound up casting a friend of mine. Still, four years later, here I am."

TIM JEROME, JENN GAMBATESE

"JANE DOESN'T FEAR TARZAN, OR MUCH OF ANYTHING ELSE, BECAUSE SHE IS ESSENTIALLY COMFORTABLE WITH NATURE. IN THAT RESPECT, SHE'S VERY MUCH LIKE TARZAN." — *TARZAN* DIRECTOR BOB CROWLEY

JENN GAMBATESE, JOSH STRICKLAND

FUN FACT: In conceiving the character of Professor Archimedes Q. Porter, Edgar Rice Burroughs was no doubt influenced at least in part by the famous history of Stanley and Livingstone. Missionary and explorer Dr. David Livingstone had not been seen in Africa for so long that it was feared he might be dead. In search of the good doctor went another adventurous soul, Henry M. Stanley, in the employ of the New York *Herald*. Stanley did locate his elusive quarry—in the town of Ujiji in present-day Tanzania—which he recounted in *How I Found Livingtone* (1871), greeting him with one of the most famous lines in English: "Dr. Livingstone, I presume?" Sir Stanley is also credited with founding the city of Léopoldville in 1881; that city is now called Kinshasa and is the capital of the Democratic Republic of the Congo.

PROFESSOR PORTER

Jane's father is a modern take on a traditional theatrical archetype, the eccentric Englishman. Here, actor Tim Jerome is pictured backstage with Jenn Gambatese (Jane) and (OPPOSITE) singing "Like No Man I've Ever Seen."

FATHERS PLAY AN ENORMOUS PART in the Broadway *Tarzan*. Tarzan's birth father is killed, and he is in constant conflict with his foster (ape) father. Jane and her father have a more functional relationship. He is named, in the original book, Archimedes Q. Porter (Archimedes being the 3rd-century Greek mathematician who jumped from his bath with a shout of 'Eureka!' when he suddenly solved the puzzle of water displacement).

"Porter starts as a stock figure," says Bob Crowley, "the eccentric Englishman—and, believe me, I know a lot of them." In the film, the role was voiced by Nigel Hawthorne, "a man of such humanity," says Crowley, "that everything he did seemed real. And I wanted some of that human reality from the Porter character in this production, too.

"Because Porter is more than just the butt of absent-minded-professor jokes," Crowley continues. "I think of him as an extraordinary man, a bit like the Brontë sisters' father, who educated his daughters when that just wasn't done. Jane is not just his daughter or even just his educated daughter. She's his colleague and collaborator; she learns from him, he from her.

"You need talent not to get lost in a stereotype when you're given the opportunity," says Crowley, "so you need a strong actor. Just as I do not want the understudies to offer up mindlessly parroted versions of the characters, I expect the actors to go back to themselves, even if they are playing an identifiable character type, and to make him or her unique.

"As I said to Tim Jerome, when Jane starts falling in love and losing her sense of perspective and getting all giddy, as you do when you fall in love, I need Porter to be a kind of anchor. He's not in love. In fact, his thoughts are probably about losing his daughter, having already lost his wife. You need to be the one who is not losing his head. I mean, he's an educated man and an adventurer. There has to be some strength, some gravitas in the man."

And Jerome couldn't have agreed more readily. "Well for one thing," the actor says, "there is a serious subtext to this story, about racism and xenophobia. I mean Clayton's attitude toward the apes is just as colonial as his attitude toward women. Porter's tolerance of his daughter's new love interest, who is a creature from another culture, is an important point of difference between Porter and Clayton."

As the second act was shaped and reshaped during the rehearsal and preview process, Professor Porter's role was in a state of constant flux. "This is something I admire actors for in general," Jerome says, "and this cast in particular, for being able to roll with that constant change, not only in rehearsal, but in performance, too."

TIM JEROME

CLAYTON

If Professor Porter represents educated man at his most benign, Clayton—the "Great White Hunter" of this safari—represents what is most unappetizing. Both the Porters love nature; Clayton sees only opportunities for enrichment. And although Clayton is more subtle, more nuanced in the show than he was in the film, he still compares unfavorably with Tarzan's innate honor and sense of decency.

Clayton, the villain of the play (originated by actor Donnie Keshawarz), is tempered by his charm, although he is still self-serving and duplicitous. THIS PAGE: Clayton with Tarzan (TOP) and Keshawarz in rehearsal with Assistant Choreographer Leonora Stapleton and Fight Director Rick Sordelet.

"Villains are difficult," says Bob Crowley, "because you can't take a villain seriously if he is standing there without any character shading, just twirling his mustache and leering." In the real world, and the best dramas, villains have motives.

"It also seemed right to me that Clayton should be from somewhere other than England, someplace else, like America. I liked the seductive quality of Clayton's Southern accent, which came naturally to Donnie Keshawarz because he grew up in Arkansas."

The very first rehearsal script, in fact, includes reference to a budding relationship between Jane and Clayton on the ship that brings them to the Congo. Which makes Clayton's behavior as a jilted lover when Tarzan wins Jane's heart a lot less delusional.

"I thought the whole Clayton subplot suggesting there had been some flirtation between Jane and Clayton—and that Jane had participated—was actually very interesting," says book writer David Henry Hwang, "but by the time you get to Tarzan meeting Jane, that's where you want to keep your focus, because that's the story."

"It certainly made it more interesting to me," says Crowley, "if Clayton is an attractive, sexy man, it means that Jane isn't just swept away by a physical infatuation with Tarzan. It's Tarzan's innocence that attracts Jane."

DONNIE KESHAWARZ

THE JUNGLE: Sights

ALL BROADWAY MUSICALS have a costume designer and a set designer, and *Tarzan* is no exception—except in this case the set and costume designer is a single individual, Bob Crowley, who is also the production's director. Since his own plate was going to be quite full, Crowley and Disney enlisted the aid of Ivo Coveney to help with the exigencies of the design for *Tarzan*.

Coveney started his career making opera props in his native England and has since contributed to such theatrical productions as *Elton John and Tim Rice's Aida, Chitty Chitty Bang Bang, Billy Elliot,* and *Mary Poppins,* as well as numerous films *(The Fifth Element, Finding Neverland, Kingdom of Heaven).* He describes himself as a "costume prop maker," and does, he says modestly, "anything that no one else wants to do." Mostly he designs and/or constructs anything that an actor wears that isn't clothing.

For example, he created the armor for Russell Crowe in *Gladiator* and the headdresses and jewelry for all three *Star Wars* prequels, among other films. On Tarzan, he's lent his skills and talents to the set, the ape costumes, and the jungle flora and fauna—even the infant Tarzan. His official title gives him credit for "Special Creatures," but around the theater he is known as the "critter guy" or the "special effects wrangler."

"Basically," he says, "Bob brought me onto the show to do anything anyone wanted to try, only some of which—like the giant moth—made it into the final show. For example, when we were down in Buenos Aires, one day Tom Schumacher said to me, 'Is it possible to have a full-sized elephant for the "Son of Man" sequence?' And the next day we bought some Styrofoam and some wood, and Pichón's guys and I mocked up a full-sized elephant. It never made it into the show, but that was the kind of thing we were doing down there, not just dealing with the flying apes.

"One of the great things about the entire Buenos Aires experience was that we didn't actually know if we were greenlit yet for a production, so there was a real sense of play in the work. The ideas were flowing. It was a very creative time."

Jane (Jenn Gambatese) gets caught in a giant spider's web, which emerges from her skirt. The costume weighs 35 pounds and takes an hour to pack for every performance. OPPOSITE: Exotic critter fabricator Ivo Coveney with his spider, his silhouetted elephant experiment, and a game actress trying out the spider web in the Buenos Aires flying workshop.

SABOR: THE LEOPARD

EVERY STORY NEEDS ITS VILLAIN, and *Tarzan* has two—one human, Clayton, and one wild, the leopard called Sabor. Sabor doesn't have any lines, but he does figure prominently in the action of the play. He kills Kala's ape baby and Tarzan's parents all in the first sequence of the show. And later he fights with Tarzan (as a great cat does in virtually every Tarzan story).

So creating Sabor was important to the production. For the most part, Sabor is played by an actor in a "costume" designed and executed by Bob Crowley and Ivo Coveney. Actually, Sabor is played by four different actors, male and female, at different times in the show: the actor inside the Sabor costume when the cat descends from the gantry into the Greystokes' tree house is not the same actor who fights with Tarzan.

But Sabor is more than a costume; he's also stage effects—one that darts across the stage to snatch up Kala's baby and another that is just shadow. Like everything else in this production, Sabor went through some significant transitions. At one point, for example, there was even an inflatable Sabor.

Coveney also credits the lighting with helping to animate his creatures. "At first I was disappointed that there wasn't more light on it," says the proud master builder, but, in fact, I now realize that the less we see it, the more menacing it seems. It's less literal when it's kept shadowy. You don't look at it and say, 'Oh, there's an actor in a leopard costume.' At least I hope you don't.

"And, of course, all of this had to be coordinated with Pichón, who was designing the way the leopard would be flying, and Dany Conde, who designed and made the harnesses, because we had to figure out how to include the actual rig in the costume that would allow the actor to move the way we wanted."

JOSH STRICKLAND, JOHN ELLIOTT OYZON

MARCUS BELLAMY

JOHN ELLIOTT OYZON

ALONG CAME A SPIDER...

IN THE ANIMATED FILM *Tarzan,* Jane's introduction to jungle life involves a disagreement over her sketch of a baby baboon and a wild ride through the jungle in Tarzan's arms while the baboon troop pursues them. It's both humorous and frightening and clearly impossible to replicate in a theater.

So Jane is not menaced by baboons in this production, but by a giant spider, another special creature created by Ivo Coveney.

"We started playing around with the spider in Argentina. We had lots of different ideas, including having the spider walk down the back wall, the way the Greystokes now do in the production. What appealed to Meryl Tankard the most was using two actors, back to back, which gives you the spider's eight limbs.

"In the production the spider is only on for one minute and forty seconds, but we didn't know that when we were figuring it out, so there were times when it was enormously complicated. At one point we were trying to make it come in upside down and flip one hundred eighty degrees, which was not so easy on the actors, I have to tell you. We never did get that working so they were comfortable.

"We worked on it some more up at Purchase, and we were fairly set with it, but then it turned out it was too big. The spider is twelve feet high, but it has to get through a space in the rigging that's only seven feet high. So we all kept offering up ideas and I kept doing drawings. I even made models, which I would show with a GI Joe so we could get the scale of the thing.

"What we wound up doing was changing from a hard shell to a series of rings held apart with cables, and we effectively just put a big hairy sack over the top that allows it to collapse. And now the deflating is actually part of the action when Tarzan swings in to rescue Jane."

To fabricate Bob Crowley's flights of fancy, the production turned to Ivo Coveney. His giant spider is manned by two ensemble members sitting back to back. OPPOSITE: Sabor in several of his many guises.

BABY T: There are two Tarzans listed in the cast of Tarzan, Young Tarzan and adult Tarzan, but there is actually a third—the squirting infant Tarzan that Kala finds in the treehouse (courtesy of "Special Creatures" fabricator Ivo Coveney). The cooing and crying voice of the infant Tarzan was provided by Ruby Oliver Shivers, the infant daughter of sound designer John Shivers.

INFANT TARZAN

COVENEY WAS ALSO RESPONSIBLE for the doll that was to represent Tarzan as an infant. As with every other aspect of the show, a good deal of collaboration went into the creation of the baby. "I worked particularly closely with Denise Grillo [Production Props]. She was great. We hit it off right away, and when it came to the baby Tarzan, her attitude was, 'Great! I'm glad you're dealing with it, because finding a good one has been a bit of a nightmare.'"

Needless to say, the doll didn't come from a toy store. Coveney sculpted it himself, after rejecting an anatomically correct baby designed to train emergency medical personnel in CPR on infants. (In fact, there's a whole catalog of rubber humans out there available for practicing mouth-to-mouth resuscitation, and Coveney keeps a library of resource material of just this kind).

"A newborn baby is actually a lot bigger than you think," he says, "and what we needed was something that was actually smaller, which, oddly, gives the impression of being the right size onstage.

"We did about seven or eight different versions of the baby, including one that was proportioned like the baby in the animated film. But that baby was drawn with an exaggeratedly large head, which looked fine in the film. It didn't work onstage."

FLORA AND FAUNA

THE JUNGLE ITSELF IS A CHARACTER in all Tarzan stories, and this one is no exception (even if the jungle is largely represented by an abstract set of green "vines"). This jungle had to be enchanting, too, particularly to Jane, for whom the world of plants is magical and the jungle enchanted.

Coveney was on hand to help with that, too, fashioning the fabulous plants and the insects that were animated by five of the ensemble members.

Kara Madrid is the ensemble member in the largest (and furthest downstage) flower. As she remembers it, the rehearsal process sometimes involved her hanging above the stage floor for extended periods of time. At one particular rehearsal, the cord that was supposed to release the petals so her flower could open (revealing her at its center) became knotted, and the supersized flower failed to open. "I was up there quite a long time, holding my pike position, while people were trying to pass me a pair of scissors through the closed petals so I could cut my way out—without damaging the flower, of course."

"At one point I was trying to design the flowers around the Hoberman sphere," says Coveney, referring to the collapsible plastic toy that is basically a construction that stays a sphere but can get bigger and smaller. "But it was too mechanical. And it was the only thing onstage that hadn't been designed specifically by us for this production. I got carried away because you don't want

MERLE DANDRIDGE

MERLE DANDRIDGE

CELINA CARVAJAL

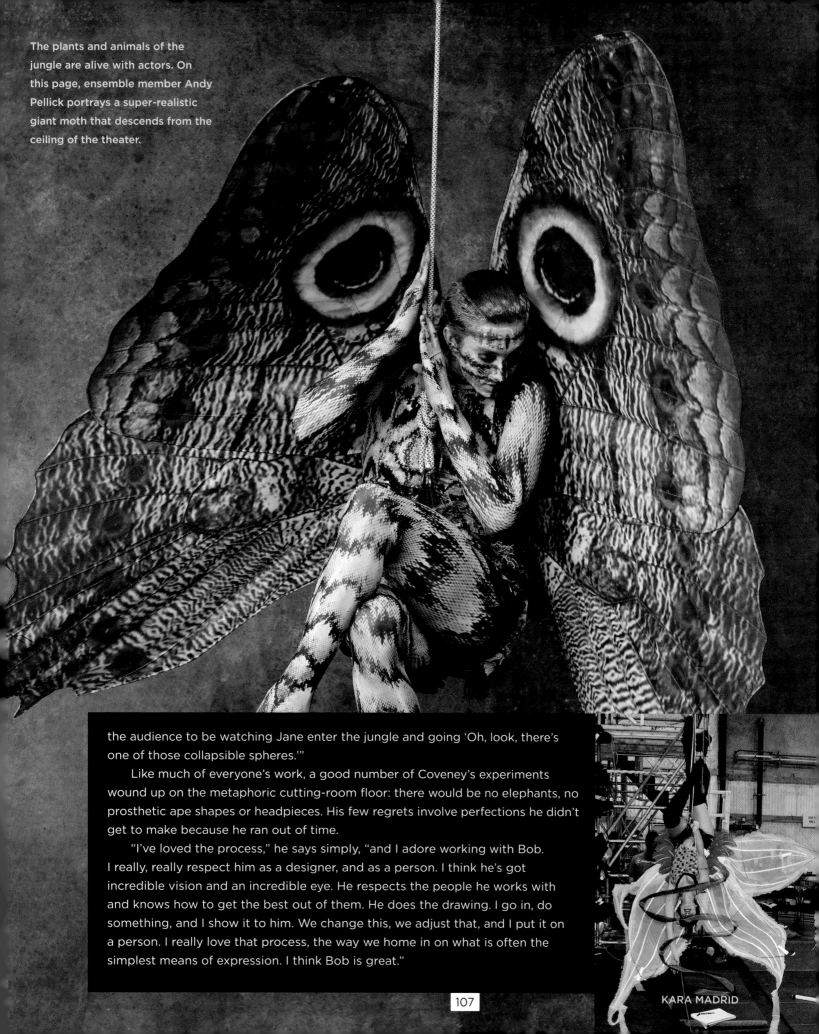

The plants and animals of the jungle are alive with actors. On this page, ensemble member Andy Pellick portrays a super-realistic giant moth that descends from the ceiling of the theater.

the audience to be watching Jane enter the jungle and going 'Oh, look, there's one of those collapsible spheres.'"

Like much of everyone's work, a good number of Coveney's experiments wound up on the metaphoric cutting-room floor: there would be no elephants, no prosthetic ape shapes or headpieces. His few regrets involve perfections he didn't get to make because he ran out of time.

"I've loved the process," he says simply, "and I adore working with Bob. I really, really respect him as a designer, and as a person. I think he's got incredible vision and an incredible eye. He respects the people he works with and knows how to get the best out of them. He does the drawing. I go in, do something, and I show it to him. We change this, we adjust that, and I put it on a person. I really love that process, the way we home in on what is often the simplest means of expression. I think Bob is great."

107

KARA MADRID

Sounds

The stage of the Richard Rodgers is filled to bursting with the set, the rigging, the lighting and sound equipment, and that's with no flying actors!

OPPOSITE: Sound designer John Shivers (RIGHT) works at the sound console with associate David Patridge.

DESIGNING SOUND for a Broadway musical is not just about balancing the orchestra and amplifying the singers—although that's important. Sound design is a complex enterprise with a serious aesthetic profile.

To design the sound for *Tarzan*, Disney hired John Shivers, whose Broadway credits include *The Lion King* and *Elton John and Tim Rice's Aida* for Disney as well as such recent shows as *Hairspray* and *The Producers,* and a half dozen more. He's designed sound for stars like Savion Glover, Dionne Warwick, Billy Crystal, and Gregory Hines.

"Sound design falls between art and science," says Shivers. "At the simplest level you have words like loud and soft, which almost everybody understands. But there is also the quality of the equalization of the highs and lows within a certain level of loud and soft. Then there's the treble and bass and midrange—the kinds of things you find on your home stereo. The equipment we've got here can basically represent the entire spectrum of frequencies that a human can hear, and we have all kinds of ways of puttIng a little polish on the sound, a little bit of reverb or echo, that kind of thing."

And, he says, "the sound design for *Tarzan* is far more sophisticated than any other production I've worked on."

In terms of hardware, that translates to more than 60 speakers and a sound system called LCS (for Level Control System), which is, in effect, surround sound. "It's a computerized system that enables us to move a sound around the speakers however we want," Shivers says. "The system uses what are called space maps, which you can design, that will move a sound from point A to point B in a certain amount of time. You can move the sound—say seagulls— clockwise through the house, or counterclockwise, or zigzag it. It gives you the very real effect that a seagull is flying around over your head.

"For this production," he says, "I wanted the sound to function as a part of the set. The set is the jungle, but there are different areas of the jungle, different sound palettes. It's the same with lighting: light looks different at dawn and at dusk; what you hear is different, too, at different times and in different situations—before and after a rainfall—and you can manipulate the sound to reinforce the mood of a scene, in the same way that music can underscore the emotional content. You can even manipulate the mood of the music."

Tarzan has hundreds of sound cues, an unusually high number, and many of those cues are tied to light cues and the score and stage action. The soundscape in the opening sequence alone, for example, has dozens of sounds, says Shivers,

Soundscape

Leading Hollywood soundman Lon Bender has created the sound for such Disney films as Mulan, Pocahontas, and The Hunchback of Notre Dame. "I used to tell Tom Schumacher when we worked together that I wanted to do sound for a Broadway show," says Bender, "and he would always say, 'Stage musicals don't need what you do.' Then one day he called me and said, 'I've got a show for you.'"

To find the sounds for Tarzan, Bender turned to the archives of his own company, Soundelux, which he founded when he was just 18, and which now has a library of some 300,000 records. The audio plot he assembled has some 200 cues, some of which are made up of 96 separate tracks. "In Jane's first scene,"

Bender says, "we wanted everything to be from her perspective, as if she and each member of the audience were the size of a bug. So that scene has flying insects and crawling insects, dirt clogs moving, grass, wind, all kinds of things."

The sound was so evocative that it came to replace the underscoring in the opening sequence. "The whole shipwreck had Phil Collins music playing along with the sound," says Bender. "Then we tried it without the music, and Bob Crowley decided it worked better without music. So this musical doesn't have any music in it for about ten minutes. It does have what is probably the most complex sound design of any show in Broadway history."

from the waves and the creaking boards to the ropes and the tackle, the sails flapping, the ship's bell, wind.

But Shivers and his team—seven during the rehearsal process, three when the show is running—do more than mix a "sound effects" track. Everything the audience hears is evaluated by the design team, and almost every sound the audience hears in *Tarzan* has been both affected and effected by the sound design, from whether sounds are loud enough to whether they are appropriate to the action. Sound is not just replicated in the world of theater design, it is both manufactured and artfully manipulated, modulated, enhanced.

As with other aspects of production, the actual sound of something may not be the sound that best serves the dramatic action. Therefore it's not the sound you want to hear. Take the first gunshot in *Tarzan,* which announces to the apes that there are humans in the jungle. "The sound you hear onstage is much louder than what you would hear in nature if a gun went off at a fair distance," says Shivers. "What you need to hear as a member of the audience is not the actual sound of a gun going off a mile away, but a theatrical sound that creates the same shock in you that the apes are experiencing onstage.

"When Kerchak roars behind Jane," Shivers continues, "that's a combination of the actor's voice and some electronic augmentation, and it's much louder than a real gorilla would likely sound. What we were going for there is Jane's experience, and, to her, that roar would be deafening."

"When Jane slaps Clayton," Shivers continues, "you wouldn't hear it past the third row if she just actually slapped him." That slap is produced by the orchestra conductor slapping his hand at the precise moment Jane's hand *seems* to be coming into contact with Clayton's face."

The whole issue of the sounds the gorillas make had to be settled early on. "I asked Bob Crowley what he wanted to do," says Shivers, "because real gorillas make grunting sounds that are a lot more like the sound we think of as coming from pigs than the noises we think a gorilla makes. We settled on a recipe that includes some gorilla, but a lot of monkey, too, which is higher pitched, and some of the actor's actual voice.

"Working on *Tarzan* has been a great process," Shivers summarizes, "a great learning experience. I mean, we've run through a gamut of issues and challenges with this show, but I think we've addressed most of them. I'm going to walk away from it feeling quite proud of the end result."

THE TARZAN YELL made its debut in the sound version of the 1928 *Tarzan and the Tiger* (which was released, like Disney's *Steamboat Willie,* in both sound and silent versions), but the high-pitched yodeling yell that most people associate with Tarzan was created by Johnny Weissmuller. He was so fond of the sound (and so given to letting loose with it in public places) that it was played at the actor's funeral as his coffin was being lowered into the ground. The Broadway Tarzan uses the yell from the sound track of the film.

JUNGLE NOISES: In 1959, producers brought trained chimpanzees with them from England to Kenya for the filming of *Tarzan's Greatest Adventure,* but the chimps were so terrified of the jungle night noises that they wouldn't perform.

FUN FACT: Phil Collins was short-listed by Italian director Franco Zeffirelli to play Romeo in his 1968 *Romeo and Juliet* opposite Olivia Hussey, then his girlfriend. Another candidate was Paul McCartney (the role went to Leonard Whiting).

THE MUSIC

Not Mount Rushmore exactly, but close (FROM LEFT): concentrated and concentrating at a rehearsal are director Bob Crowley, producer Thomas Schumacher, composer/lyricist Phil Collins, and music producer Paul Bogaev.

JUNGLES ARE NOT QUIET PLACES, and neither are Broadway musicals set in the jungle. The music staff for *Tarzan* included a music producer, a music director (both of whom doubled as arrangers), an orchestrator, a music coordinator, an associate music director (doubling as rehearsal pianist), a pair of music copyists, a synthesizer programmer (and an assistant for same), a resident percussionist/drum arranger, a music production assistant, and a dozen of Broadway's best pit musicians.

But the story of the music for this show centers on an internationally acclaimed singer, songwriter, and drummer named Phil Collins and his debut as the writer of music and lyrics for a stage musical.

The native Londoner wasn't actually planning to write a Broadway musical, but who better than Collins could Disney have asked to compose this one? After all, the famed recording artist had written—and sung— the songs in the hit animated *Tarzan* film. In the process, he won a Grammy® for the double-platinum sound track album and a "Best Song" Oscar® and a Golden Globe® for "You'll Be in My Heart."

The Broadway *Tarzan* would need a lot of new music and all of the extant music would have to be reset. The best way to make sure that the new score met the film's standard, was to go to the source. The source, of course, has been entertaining people for decades. He has had numerous platinum and gold records and, in the 1980s, could boast a string of U.S. Top Ten singles, from "You Can't Hurry Love" and "One More Night" to "Another Day in Paradise." His first two Oscar® nominations were for "Against All Odds," from the film of the same name, and "Two Hearts" from *Buster,* in which he also starred in the title role.

Besides, reports Thomas Schumacher, the producer had thoroughly enjoyed working with Collins on the animated film *Tarzan* and welcomed the opportunity to extend their professional relationship. Phil Collins may not have needed another adventure in his musical life, but when the jungle path was open before him, he chose to take it, much to his producer's satisfaction.

"I viewed this as a perfect opportunity to spread my musical wings and widen my horizons," says Collins. "Besides, I'm just not the kind of person to let someone else take over," he continues. "You can decide for yourself if that's artistic commitment or a control issue. For me it was an opportunity to do something and to see it through properly."

In the spirit of collaboration, however, Collins did not restrict his input to matters musical. "Phil was instrumental in shaping this show," says Schumacher. "He was with us during the readings and workshops, through

FUN FACT: Phil Collins made his recording debut with a self-penned number called "Lying Crying Dying," with a band called The Freehold. His first album, "Ark 2," was recorded with Flaming Youth in 1969.

111

THOMAS SCHUMACHER, PHIL COLLINS (ABOVE AND RIGHT)

singing on Broadway. And as much as I love Ethel Merman, that is not the kind of voice these songs wanted."

Affable and self-effacing, especially about theatrical issues, Collins developed an easy rapport with Bob Crowley, although the musician was nervous about meeting him. "I was brought up in the theater," says Collins, who debuted in the original production of Lionel Bart's *Oliver!* in London's West End when he was still a teenager, "but I'm not an intellectual particularly, and here I was meeting the designer and director. I was a bit intimidated.

"It turned out that the original set for *Oliver!* had had a big impact on Bob, so we had that in common, and we hit it off right away."

"Phil Collins is a great musician," says Crowley, "but his attitude right from the beginning was, 'You know more about theater than I do, let me learn from you.'" And that sense of everyone learning together extended to the entire company.

auditions and callbacks and the whole rehearsal process."

"Phil functioned exactly the way a Broadway composer like Richard Rodgers functioned back in the day," says Music Director Jim Abbott. "He would sit at the drum set during rehearsals and help teach the songs to the ensemble. He was there working all the time." He even attended auditions. "Well," Collins says, "I wanted to make sure that the voices were right for the music. I mean, there's quite a range of

Collins was also able to work fluidly with book writer David Henry Hwang. The two were continually called on to rewrite scenes at a moment's notice, and to negotiate whether the plot point under discussion should be carried by words, music, or both.

FUN FACT: When Phil Collins was in *Oliver!* the role of Fagin was played by Barry Humphries (better known to the world now as Dame Edna Everage).

"David came up with a lot of ideas," says Collins freely. "I'd say, 'When a big song comes up, I want to know what you think, because you're writing what's before it and after it. Give me some ideas of what you want said in this song.' And he'd always come up with a few things."

"This was the best collaboration I've ever had," says *Tarzan*'s Music Producer Paul Bogaev, who has served as music producer, supervisor, director, arranger, or orchestrator for many television and film projects as well as such Broadway musicals as *Elton John and Tim Rice's Aida*. He's won Grammy® awards for the cast albums of *Aida* and *Chicago* and an Emmy® for his musical direction of *Annie*.

"He's absolutely as perfectionist and meticulous as anybody that I've worked with," says Bogaev, "but he doesn't have an unrealistic temperament, which is rare. He has a mature temperament. So, if he gets upset, it's usually because somebody has not been doing his job. And he's completely justified in that because he does what a lot of people in his

position don't do: he really does work. He doesn't leave it to others.

"Plus," Bogaev continues, "he can sing. How many times do you do a Broadway show and have the composer on hand to sing the songs? He doesn't do it so people will copy him—he didn't want that at all. But there's an honesty in the way he sings through the music that you have to hear. He has a great innate sense of melody and he's not an embellisher. So you don't want to try to copy the way he sounds, but you do want to capture the way he connects to the music.

The Broadway *Tarzan* score includes all five songs from the film, nine additional songs, and considerable new underscoring. One of the songs, "I Need to Know," sung by Young Tarzan, was originally written for *Tarzan II*. Furthermore, the stage version gives the composer the opportunity to air his songs at the length he wrote them. Before the *Tarzan* film, Collins jokes, he was unfamiliar with the "efficiency" of an animated film song. "Ninety seconds and you're in and out," he says.

It's a collaborative world, after all. OPPOSITE: The producer and composer listen together. THIS PAGE, FROM TOP: Composer (Phil Collins) and director/designer (Bob Crowley); title actor (Josh Strickland) and composer (Phil Collins); music director (Jim Abbott, at keyboard) with actress (Merle Dandridge), composer (Phil Collins) and music producer Paul Bogaev in Brooklyn.

"One of the things I've learned," says Phil Collins, "is that you can have a great song, but if it's not right for the character or the scene, or even the actor—or if it's in the wrong place— then it's not doing its job, so walk away with your head held high."

Gary Seligson, the production's resident percussionist, is also effusive in his assessment of Collins. "When Phil writes, he hears the songs as a drummer. His melodies are really grounded, yet they're extremely syncopated. I mean listen to 'Sure As Sun Turns to Moon.' The percussion is so beautiful, so intricate, and the parts fit together like gears in a clock."

One of the major differences between writing for film and writing for the stage is that when Collins composed the film, he knew he was going to be singing the songs. He knew that he was writing the new stage songs for other performers. "It's one thing to write for myself," says Collins, "but a great deal of the charm of the theater is seeing how characters reveal themselves in their songs. So I have to be writing for other characters as well as other voices. But that's also part of the fun of it."

"Some of the songs are script-driven," says Collins, citing as an example, "Waiting for This Moment," the song Jane sings on her entrance. Her Act II song, "For the First Time," had a different evolution.

"I always felt that Jane should have a song where she expresses what it's like to be in love with Tarzan. So I just wrote a love song that wasn't in the script. I wrote it as a song for me but from a female point of view. Everybody loved it, and then Bob Crowley said, 'Wouldn't it be lovely if, unbeknownst to Jane, Tarzan was in another place singing the same thing?'

"I couldn't see it any other way other than Jane's song, but we tried it as a parallel duet, and it gets one of the best audience receptions in the show. That was just one of the examples of the collaboration on this show. How it winds up is everybody's idea, no matter who thought of it first."

On the other hand, Collins allows, there is such a thing as delegating. There are times, for example, when arranging and orchestrating are nearly synonymous with composing. Doug Besterman did the orchestrations for *Tarzan*; dance arrangements are credited to Music Director Jim Abbott and vocal arrangements to Music Producer Paul Bogaev.

"There are times when I've written something on the computer," and I have no idea how to turn it into something someone can play," says Collins. And Jim or Paul would go off and come back and play something for me that he'd written, and it'd be great. And it's based on what I wrote and sounds like something like it, but it's much, much better."

"I can't tell you how great he's been," says music director Jim Abbott, who has previously filled the same job for *Elton John and Tim Rice's Aida, Rent*, and *Bombay Dreams*, among other productions, and played keyboards for *Footloose, Cats, Miss Saigon*, and *The Who's Tommy*, as well

as for soloists Aretha Franklin, Shirley Bassey, Bob Hope, Vanessa Williams, and Elton John.

"He's someone who really cares. He's always examining, and he never blows off anything. And he wants you to be creative. The first thing I actually wrote for the show that wasn't his was the back half of the dance sequence right before Jane's entrance, which is gone now. But I remember, I kind of just demo'ed it, and I said to him, 'Look, this is just a placeholder. You can do whatever you

want here."' And he said, 'No, I really like it.' He cares much more about the sound of the show than he cares about his own ego."

Part of the complexity of perfecting the music for *Tarzan* is that Collins does not read music. He composes on a computer, a big computer with access to whole libraries of sounds. Those demos, say both Abbott and Seligson, are like no other demos in the business. And it was part of the music team's job to translate what they could hear on Collins's audio tracks into music notation.

"Phil doesn't put anything on paper," says Jim Abbott. It's all just audio, or MIDI, which is Musical

Instrument Digital Interface, a data format for computers and keyboards. That's what Phil uses to compose. So we got all these MIDI files from Phil, and Ethan Popp, the associate conductor, and I sat there in a room with a MIDI file and the audio and my sequencer, which I set up to be just like Phil's sequencer, with a bigger sampler, and we sat there and we transcribed every little line that Phil put in the thing."

THIS PAGE: Phil Collins in his studio. OPPOSITE: Collins, with (FROM LEFT): Thomas Schumacher, Disney Music's Chris Montan, Pichón Baldinu, Paul Bogaev, Jim Abbott, and David Henry Hwang.

PHIL COLLINS, CHRIS MONTAN, PAUL BOGAEV

THIS PAGE: Resident percussionist Gary Seligson jams with Phil Collins (ABOVE) and Horace V. Rogers offers up "Son of Man" at a rehearsal. OPPOSITE: Tarzan and Jane (Josh Strickland and Jenn Gambatese) fall in love singing at the New 42nd Street Studios.

"With this score," says Seligson, "Phil had a fully developed concept of what the percussion should be. So at first a lot of the job was just listening to his demos and figuring out how to get that sound live in the theater. How many people would it take? What could be electronic, what would be live? Because we don't even have room in the pit for everything we'd need to do it all live. And it may sound like there are six percussionists down there, but there are only three."

Being in on the myriad decisions—from major conceptual issues to the minutiae of percussion transcription—is why Collins insisted on being on site. "If I had just sent in a batch of songs and stayed home in Geneva," he imagines, "a lot of what I love about the score might never have happened. I mean, someone would have called me up and said, for example, that one

of the songs I'd grown so attached to didn't work for the show anymore. And I'd say, 'Are you sure you've tried it properly?' If I'm at the rehearsals, I can hear what's wrong with it or what's right with it, and I can do what needs to happen."

"One of the most beautiful things that I'll take away from this process," says Gary Seligson, "was being in the music room at Steiner Studios, where Jim and Paul were teaching vocals to the cast. So we'd have the 20 people sitting there, learning the parts. And Phil would walk in, and he would just be kind of listening, and tapping his feet. Drumming his fingers on his chest. Just grooving, singing a line occasionally."

One of Jim Abbott's favorite memories from working on the show comes from the recording session for the cast album. "So we were recording the album," Abbott remembers, "and Phil just can't stay in the control room. He has to get out on the floor and play percussion. He just loved to be in it that much. He brings that attitude to the process: You do it because you love it."

"It's amazing how naïve about the process I really was," admits Collins. "I thought I'd come here and we would just rehearse what we'd already decided on. I had no idea," he adds laughing. "My friends said, 'Oh, you'll be so bored just sitting and listening and watching the same thing over and over.' I had no idea that what you hand in before the first rehearsal is just the place you start."

So given all the things he's learned, would he do it again? "I'd love to write another Broadway musical," Collins says without hesitation. "I would start another one tomorrow."

FUN FACT: The haunting bonus track on the *Tarzan* cast album—"Everything That I Am," sung by Phil Collins—is actually his original demo for the song.

JOSH STRICKLAND

MISSION ACCOMPLISHED IV

I WILL PROTECT YOU FROM ALL AROUND YOU
I WILL BE HERE
DON'T YOU CRY
(FROM "YOU'LL BE IN MY HEART")

MERLE DANDRIDGE

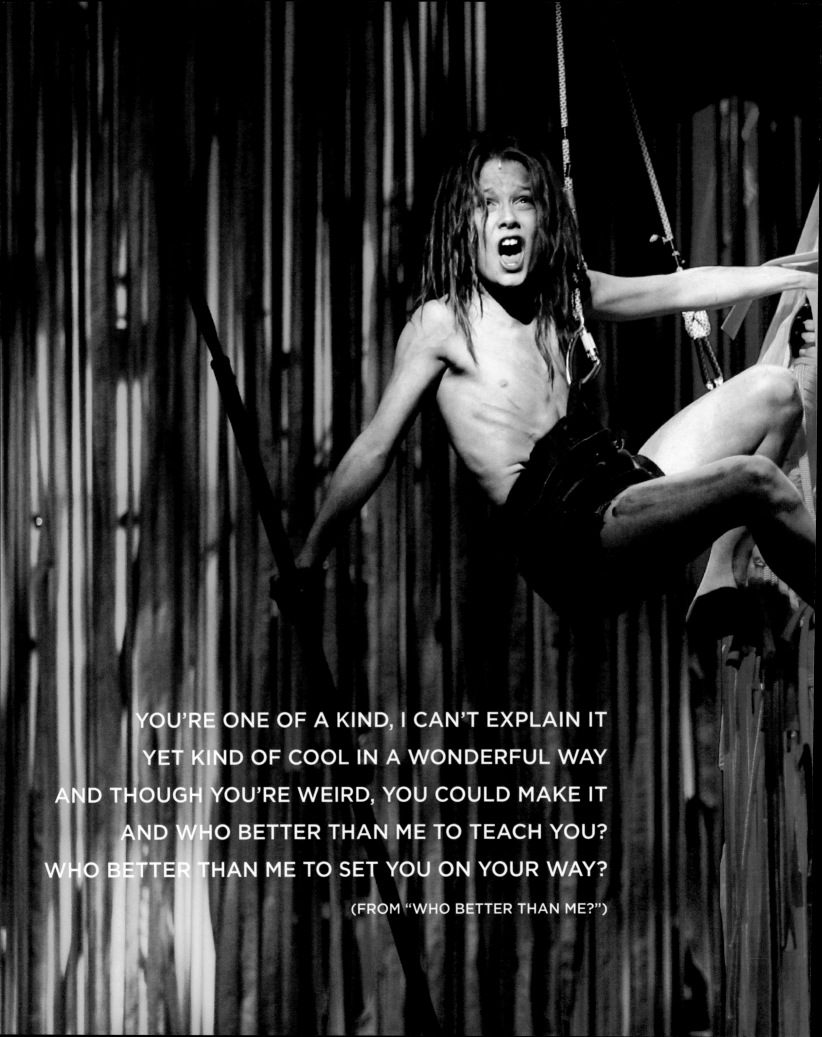

YOU'RE ONE OF A KIND, I CAN'T EXPLAIN IT
YET KIND OF COOL IN A WONDERFUL WAY
AND THOUGH YOU'RE WEIRD, YOU COULD MAKE IT
AND WHO BETTER THAN ME TO TEACH YOU?
WHO BETTER THAN ME TO SET YOU ON YOUR WAY?

(FROM "WHO BETTER THAN ME?")

ALEX RUTHERFORD, CHESTER GREGORY II

HE WON'T COME BETWEEN ME
AND THOSE I LOVE

BELIEVE ME WHEN I SAY

WITH MY BODY AND SOUL,
THIS I VOW

NO! NO OTHER WAY

IN SPITE OF YOUR PAIN
IT WILL BE DONE

NO MATTER
WHAT YOU SAY

HE NEVER WAS OR
COULD BE, BE MY SON

THERE IS NO
OTHER WAY

(FROM "NO OTHER WAY")

MERLE DANDRIDGE, SHULER HENSLEY

MERLE DANDRIDGE, ALEX RUTHERFORD

WILL SOMEONE TELL ME WHERE I BELONG

WHERE I SHOULD GO?

CAN SOMEONE TELL ME WHERE I'M GOING WRONG?

I NEED TO KNOW

WHY WOULD I HURT THE ONES I LOVE?

(FROM "I NEED TO KNOW")

KALA: IT'S NICE TO SEE YOU SMILING AND LAUGHING

KERCHAK: WHAT DO YOU MEAN? I DO IT ALL THE TIME

(FROM "SURE AS SUN TURNS TO MOON")

MERLE DANDRIDGE, SHULER HENSLEY

JOSH STRICKLAND, JOHN ELLIOTT OYZON

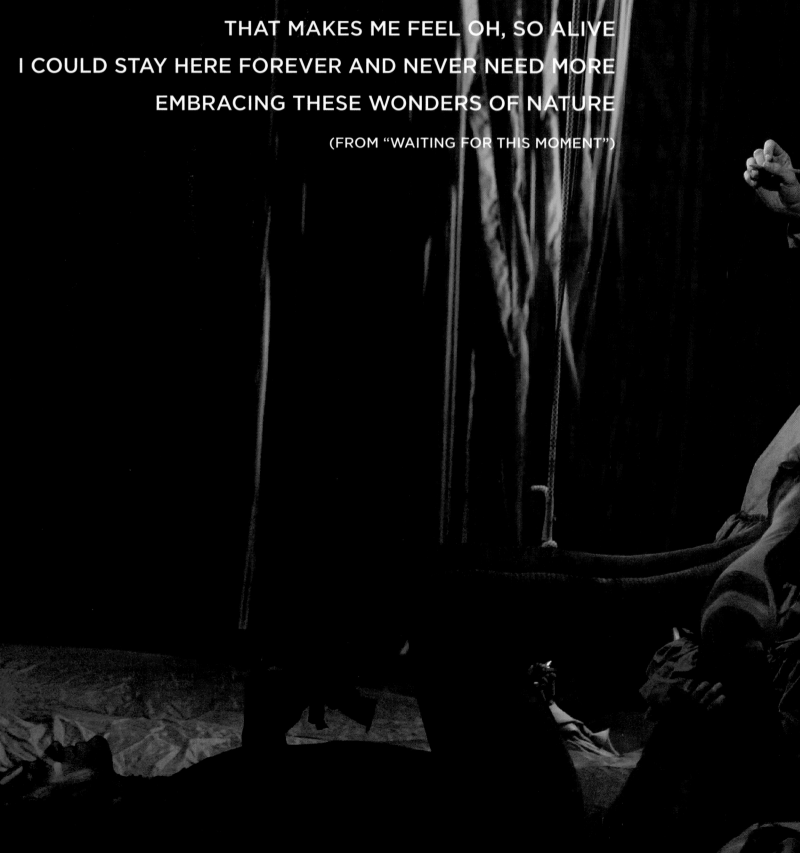

THERE'S SOMETHING STRANGELY INTOXICATING

AND IT'S GOING TO MY HEAD

THAT MAKES ME FEEL OH, SO ALIVE

I COULD STAY HERE FOREVER AND NEVER NEED MORE

EMBRACING THESE WONDERS OF NATURE

(FROM "WAITING FOR THIS MOMENT")

JENN GAMBATESE

JENN GAMBATESE, JOSH STRICKLAND

IT'S JUST LIKE ME, YET IT'S SO DIFFERENT
WHERE DID THIS COME FROM?
THESE THINGS IT'S GOT HERE ARE OH, SO DIFFERENT
WHERE DOES IT BELONG

(FROM "DIFFERENT")

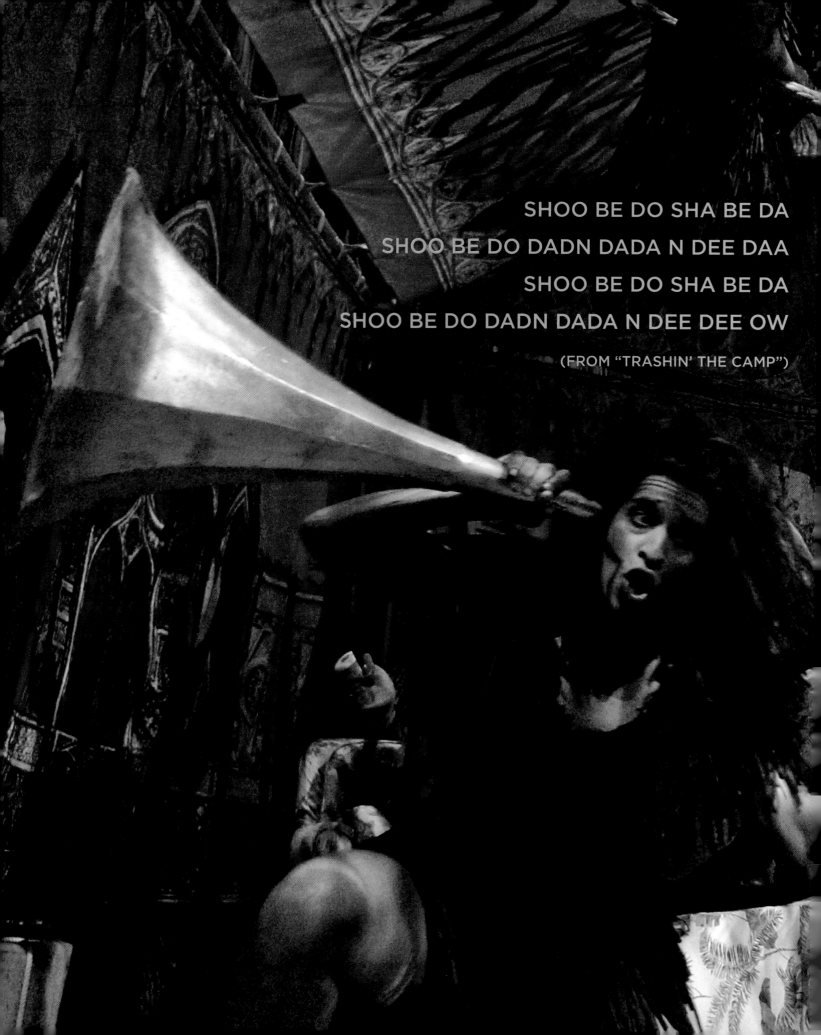

SHOO BE DO SHA BE DA

SHOO BE DO DADN DADA N DEE DAA

SHOO BE DO SHA BE DA

SHOO BE DO DADN DADA N DEE DEE OW

(FROM "TRASHIN' THE CAMP")

JENN GAMBATESE, JOSH STRICKLAND

I WANNA KNOW, CAN YOU SHOW ME?
I WANNA KNOW ABOUT THESE STRANGERS LIKE ME
TELL ME MORE, PLEASE SHOW ME
SOMETHING'S FAMILIAR ABOUT THESE STRANGERS LIKE ME

(FROM "STRANGERS LIKE ME")

JENN GAMBATESE, JOSH STRICKLAND

COME WITH ME NOW TO SEE MY WORLD

WHERE THERE'S BEAUTY BEYOND YOUR DREAMS

CAN YOU FEEL THE THINGS I FEEL RIGHT NOW, WITH YOU?

TAKE MY HAND

THERE'S A WORLD YOU NEED TO KNOW

(FROM "STRANGERS LIKE ME")

MERLE DANDRIDGE, JOSH STRICKLAND, TIM JEROME

NO ONE COULD UNDERSTAND THE WAY WE FEEL

HOW WOULD THEY KNOW, HOW CAN WE EXPLAIN?

ALTHOUGH WE'RE DIFFERENT, DEEP INSIDE US

WE'RE NOT THAT DIFFERENT AT ALL

(FROM "YOU'LL BE IN MY HEART")

MERLE DANDRIDGE, JOSH STRICKLAND

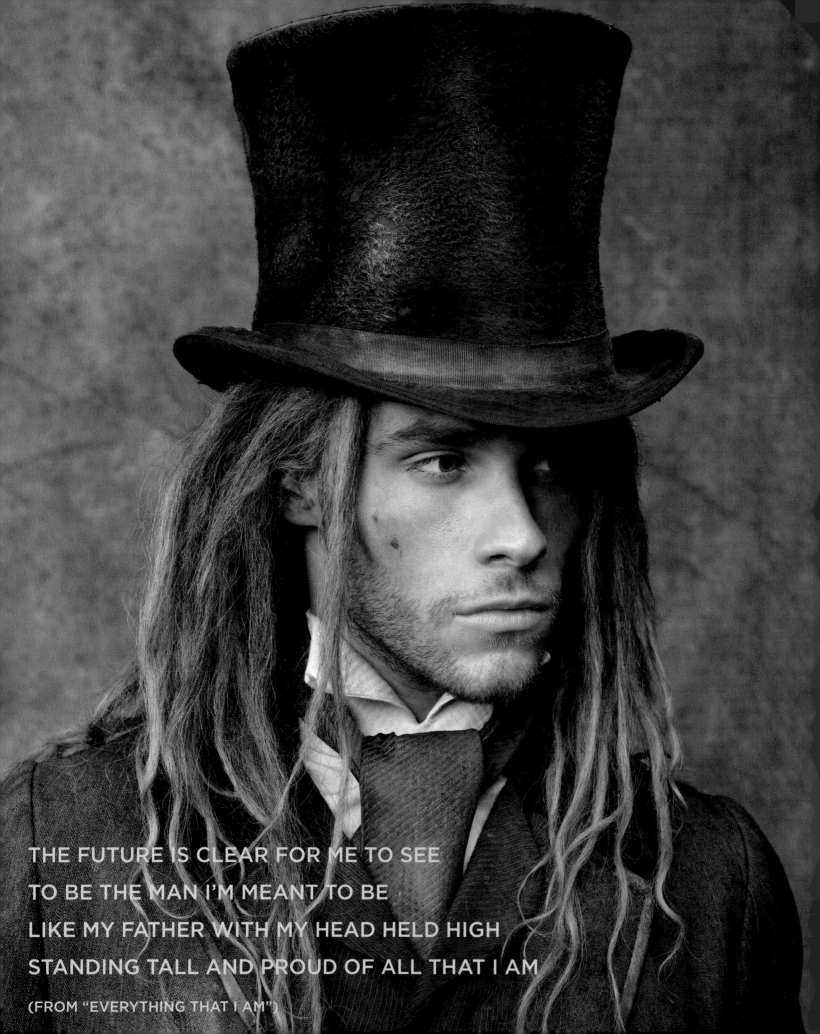

THE FUTURE IS CLEAR FOR ME TO SEE
TO BE THE MAN I'M MEANT TO BE
LIKE MY FATHER WITH MY HEAD HELD HIGH
STANDING TALL AND PROUD OF ALL THAT I AM

(FROM "EVERYTHING THAT I AM")

JOSH STRICKLAND (BOTH PAGES)

WITH EVERY ENDING COMES A NEW BEGINNING

TWO WORLDS ONE FAMILY

(FROM "TWO WORLDS")

JENN GAMBATESE, JOSH STRICKLAND

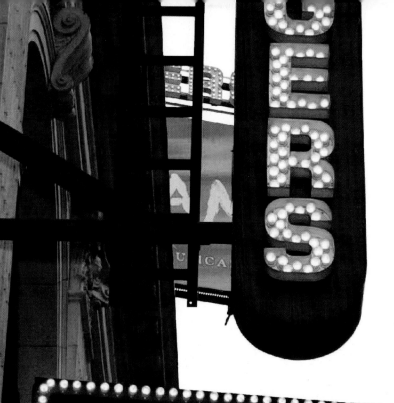

A New Beginning

EPILOGUE

To anyone who works in the performing arts, there are few sounds more satisfying than the ovation of an audience who approves of what they have just seen, and as the stage lights went out on the finale of the opening night performance of *Tarzan*®, the audience made its approval known. After months of hard work and years of preparation, *Tarzan* was now fully public, and emotions ran high backstage and in the dressing rooms that stack atop one another in the wing space up to the catwalk.

If nothing else, opening night is always a relief. However you got there, you have crossed the finish line.

There was a party, too, in the ballroom of a nearby hotel, where the close-knit company of *Tarzan* had a well-deserved chance to relax, celebrate, eat, rehash, reminisce, dance, and meet each other's wives and boyfriends, mothers, aunts, brothers, and children. It was show family meeting family of origin—Broadway style. Everything was poised to come up roses.

But as we all know, real dangers lurk in even the most enchanted forest. The *Tarzan* company wouldn't be fully out of the woods until the overnight reviews came in. Would the New York critics, with their millions of readers, viewers, and listeners, be the sharp-fanged hyenas or kindly woodsmen of this denouement?

Among the creative team, and especially the producers of Disney Theatrical Productions, there was trepidation. Broadway shows are multimillion-dollar enterprises, so producers are invariably on pins and needles after an opening night. Disney has an uneasy history with New York City's theater critics.

Reviews of Disney's shows by the Manhattan-based press have never been unreservedly positive. The critical response to *Beauty and the Beast*, Disney's first outing on Broadway (and now one of the longest-running shows in Broadway history), was downright negative. Press for *The Lion King* was broadly positive, but reserved, if not mixed. In some cases, the women and men charged with evaluating the production seemed grudging, even resentful, that they were forced to admit that a Disney show had stage merit. But *The Lion King* certainly was not the occasion for unbridled critical acclaim that some now choose to remember.

Elton John and Tim Rice's Aida, the third Disney outing on the Great White Way, was also roundly panned by the New York City press. *Aida* ran for four years on Broadway, and all of these shows have had multiple productions on the road and abroad. For those on the Disney team, it has been hard not to feel just a little underwhelmed by the "welcome" shown by the Broadway establishment. Conspiracy theorists would have no trouble believing that the drama wing of the local media had a collective axe to grind.

Now, good press, it is generally believed, cannot long help a bad show. Eventually word of mouth will kill the run. But, often, bad press can shut down a production that deserves a longer life. This is less true than it once was, but *The New York Times* still has a significant impact on attendance, particularly because it is read by so many people outside of Manhattan. And so the opinion of the *Times* critic comes to matter whether he is absolutely correct or incomprehensively wide of the mark in his evaluation.

Sadly, the early reviews of *Tarzan* were not generally positive. Some were insultingly dismissive, as if all the work and talent that had gone into the show were nothing more than an annoying insect to be flicked away on a summer night. Others roiled with a force of rhetorical hyperbole it was hard to imagine justifying. This was, after all, an entertainment—a relatively modest and somewhat experimental entertainment—and it wasn't pretending to be anything more. Some reviewers, as usual, even managed to misstate some points of fact and to misrepresent others.

The cast, the crew, and the entire creative team took a deep breath. Was this *Tarzan* they were reading about the same show they had been working on for months, or years? Did this show of the daily reviewers even exist? Because something seemed to be pleasing audiences at the Richard Rodgers Theater.

Self-doubt, as we all know, is one of the most potentially debilitating emotions we face as human beings. On the other hand, self-reflection gives us the chance to renew, recharge, and recommit. The future of *Tarzan* hung not in the balance of journalistic opionion but in the way the company reacted to *Tarzan*'s press.

The high energy and good feeling that had pervaded every aspect of the production process took a little nap. The mood backstage grew quieter and more introspective—although the crowds of fans, shutterbugs, and autograph seekers at the stage door did not diminish. To their credit, the cast did not react with anger, bitterness, depression, self-justification, or blame. Instead, they turned to each other for support. They put on their makeup and costumes and went out on stage to give the best performances they knew how to give.

And they listened to their audiences, not just at the final curtain but all the way through the show—audiences that contained a large number of young people. Even before more positive reviews began to reach the theater, the *Tarzan* company had rebounded in full force. With a shrug to the naysayers they simply went about the business of entertaining the ticket-buying public.

Happily, additional reviews began to accrue later in the week. While not all were glowing, at least the reviewers managed to find some aspects of the production that spoke to them. Richard Zoglin of *Time* magazine, for example, was struck by the set and the flying, noting that "Bob Crowley's design—lush vine forests, undulating waters, shape-shifting plants—and the aerial choreography, from the creator of off-Broadway's De La Guarda troupe, *make it the most visually enthralling show since The Lion King."

Writing in the *Financial Times,* Brendan Lemon, too, expressed admiration for the physical production, exclaiming, "What stagecraft! Bob Crowley, who directed as well as designed the sets and costumes, is a wizard," going on to summarize that "Tarzan is the only show of the season that places us joyously in a world of wonder. "

Finally, thought the cast and company! Some validation of their own perception—or at least of their hopes, dreams, and painstaking hours of rehearsal. They weren't crazy, after all. Or, if they were, there were others who enjoyed their folly.

In *Variety,* David Rooney wrote, "The emotional themes are universal ones—parental loss, mother-son attachment, the quest for paternal approval, the struggle with identity, the discovery of love. There's also the eternal conundrum of man's relationship to the natural world. Particularly in the second act…[David Henry] Hwang has shaped a show that's kid-friendly but has sufficient warm sentimentality to move adults."

Frank Scheck of *The Hollywood Reporter* noted "A gorgeous and imaginative production," praising the show's "series of dazzling stage images that have a significant 'wow' effect." Wendell Brock of The Atlanta Journal-Constitution described the production as a "gaspingly beautiful design achievement that uses aerial choreography and a dazzling bag of optical tricks to plunge the viewer deep into the vortex of its…tale in an opening scene that will be talked about for years to come."

And Europe agreed. From England came Charles Spencer's assessment for the *London Telegraph:* "The opening minutes of Tarzan…are among the most exciting and inventive I have ever witnessed in the theatre." Spencer also found the movement work compelling: "Thanks to Meryl Tankard's athletic tumbling choreography," he wrote, "and Pichón Baldinu's stunning aerial stunts, the show creates a sense of wonder and delight. the relationship between Tarzan and the apes is touchingly caught. This is a classic Disney narrative of a central character desperately trying to discover who he is."

Howard Shapiro's experience of the show was reported in *The Philadelphia Inquirer,* in which he called the production "an eye-popping treat of lighting, streamers and fabrics, in which Bob Crowley's scenery is as fluid as the actors who wear his fanciful costumes and move to his frisky direction.…Tarzan is at its best," he wrote, "when the apes are artfully wrecking a campsite, or when Tarzan is bounding across and above the stage, trying to find his way in life, in any one of Phil Collins's playful…songs."

Shapiro went on to praise individual members of the cast, noting in particular that Josh Strickland "sends out all the perfect signals for a Disney Tarzan—he's a positive guy who figures out who he is who he must be, and goes for it. He's a

Tarzan you would want your kids to ape, in a production that says: It's a jungle out there, but while you're in here, at least be entertained."

AND ONE MORE SHORT FLASH FORWARD

In the second full week of performances after the opening, the *Tarzan* cast and crew gathered at the Richard Rodgers Theater for a catered picnic supper in the lobby, after which they repaired to the theater for the first playing of the *Tarzan* Broadway cast album.

Josh Strickland and Jenn Gambatese sat near the front of the house, but backwards, facing the seats, not the stage. The two boys who play Young Tarzan sat with them. The rest of the cast and company sat in the orchestra, facing the stage, in no order whatsoever: actor, drummer, stagehand, director, electrician.

The sound quality in the house was terrific, of course, thanks to sound designer John Shivers's deployment of speakers for the show, but what was most heartening was the attitude, the behavior of the cast. As each track played, the actors who were singing crept under the metaphoric carpet, as if embarrassed (however secretly happy they may have been). And after each track, everyone else in the cast applauded warmly. Beaming smiles flashed around the theater from person to person in a meteor shower of shared memories and affections. There was something about it of the best moments you can have in high school.

The final track of the album is the Phil Collins bonus track, his recording of "Everything That I Am," which is the song written for Tarzan in which he accepts his identity as a human: "I am a man." As the last chord of it faded in the house, the cast was wrapped in its message and their own emotions. They seemed almost reluctant to offer their applause to Collins, a man most of them had come to love, who was, as usual, in the house.

It was as if everyone in the company had gone through a test and had passed it by ignoring negativity and embracing the best parts of themselves, their work, and their production. And as the mood was finally broken by applause, chatter, and the stage manager's booming call of "half hour," the company of *Tarzan* had proved itself a family, too.

Brought together by circumstance, they had worked together, learned together, grown together. Although there were differences in age, size, race, class, gender, ethnicity, national origin, religion, and native language, they had shared common experiences, had supported and helped each other. Had been responsible for one another's safety. Had encouraged each other. Had performed together, broken bread together, laughed and cried together. They had faced a seemingly united hostile force and trusted each other to do the best each of them could individually. They had forged the very bond that *Tarzan* is all about.

And as they retreated to their individual dressing rooms to get ready for the evening performance, each of them knew that it was together, as a family of the voluntary kind, that they would succeed, survive, teach, and enjoy.

FADE OUT, VOICEOVER: TARZAN'S TRIUMPHANT YELL!

Opening Night: May 10, 2006
Richard Rodgers Theater
Under the Direction of James M. Nederlander and
James L. Nederlander

STAFF FOR *TARZAN®*

Project Manager ....LIZBETH CONE
Assistant to Associate Producer .... Emily B. Powell
Show Accountant.............................. Jodi Yeager

COMPANY MANAGER.............................RANDY MEYER
Associate Company Manager ....Eduardo Castro

Assistant Choreographer ....Leonora Stapleton
Assistant Aerial Designer .... Angela Phillips

"Son of Man" Animated Sequence ....
....Little Airplane Productions, Inc.

GENERAL PRESS REPRESENTATIVE
BONEAU/BRYAN-BROWN........................ Chris Boneau
............................Jim Byk, Matt Polk, Juliana Hannett

Production Stage Manager .... Clifford Schwartz
Stage Manager............................... Frank Lombardi
Assistant Stage Managers .... Julia P. Jones
.... Tanya Gillette
.... Robert M. Armitage
Dance Captain............................... Marlyn Ortiz
Assistant Dance Captain .... Stefan Raulston
Fight Captain... Stefan Raulston
Production Assistants ....Ryan J. Bell
....Sara Bierenbaum

Associate Scenic Designer .... Brian Webb
Scenic Design Associate .... Rosalind Coombes
Assistant Scenic Designer ....Frank McCullough
Associate Costume Designer .... Mary Peterson
Assistant Costume Designer ....Daryl Stone
Associate Lighting Designer...................Yael Lubetzky
Assistant Lighting Designer.................... Aaron Spivey
Automated Lighting Programmer ....
.... Aland Henderson
Automated Lighting Tracker........................Jesse Belsky
Assistant to Lighting Designer ....Richard Swan
Associate Sound Designer .... David Patridge

Assistant Sound Designer.............................Jeremy Lee
LCS Sound System Programmer...........Garth Hemphill
"Son of Man" Visual Development............Kevin Harkey
Hand Lettering of Show Scrim..
.....................................Harriet Rose Calligraphy & Design

Technical Supervisor .... Tom Shane Bussey
Associate Technical Supervisor.............Rich Cocchiara
Assistant Technical Supervisor .... Matt Richman
Technical Production Assistant ....Noelle Font
Production Carpenter................................ Jeff Goodman
Assistant Carpenter ....Mike Kearns
Assistant Carpenter/Foy Operator.........Richard Force
Scenic Automation ....Dave Brown
Deck Automation .... Mike Fedigan
Assistant Carpenter .... Kirk Aengenheyster
Assistant Carpenter ....Will Carey
Assistant Carpenter ....Paul Curran
Assistant Carpenter ....Thorvald Jacobson
Harness Construction .... Dany Conde
Production Electrician............................. Jimmy Fedigan
Head Electrician/Light Board Operator ....
.... Randy Zaibek
Lead Follow Spot Operator ....Andrew Dean
Moving Light Technician...............................Derek Healy
Pyrotechnician ....Norman Ballard
Production Props ....Denise Grillo
Assistant Props .... Kevin Crawford
Props Shopper ....Kate Foster
Production Sound .... David Patridge
Sound Engineer ....Phil Lojo
Atmospheric Effects ....Chic Silber
Associate to Mr. Silber................................. Aaron Waitz
Wardrobe Supervisor .... Nanette Golia
Assistant Wardrobe Supervisor.............Margaret Kurz
Dressers .... Vivienne Crawford, Jay Gill,
.... Margo Lawless, Lisa Preston,
.... Melanie McClintock, Linda Zimmerman
Hair Supervisor ....Gary Martori
Assistant Supervisor ....Valerie Galdstone
Hairdresser.....................................Charlene Belmond
Makeup Supervisor...................................Angela Johnson
Assistant Makeup Supervisor ....Jorge Vargas

Music Copyist ....Russell Anixter, Donald Rice/
..................................Anixter Rice Music Service
Synthesizer Programmer ....Andrew Barrett
Synthesizer Programmer Assistant... Anders Boström
Electronic Drum Arrangements.............. Gary Seligson
Rehearsal Drummer ....Gary Seligson
Rehearsal Pianist .... Ethan Popp

Music Production Assistant...............Brian Allan Hobbs

ORCHESTRA
Conductor — Jim Abbott
Associate Conductor — Ethan Popp
Synthesizer Programmer — Andrew Barrett

Keyboard I: Jim Abbott; Keyboard 2: Ethan Popp;
Keyboard 3: Martyn Axe;
Drums: Gary Seligson; Percussion: Roger Squitero,
Javier Diaz; Bass: Hugh Mason; Guitar: JJ McGeehan;
Cello: Jeanne LeBlanc; Flutes; Anders Boström;
Reeds: Charles Pillow; Trumpet: Anthony Kadleck;
Trombone: Bruce Eidem; French Horn: Theresa
MacDonnell

Music Coordinator: Michael Keller

BERNARD TELSEY CASTING, C.S.A.
Bernie Telsey, Will Cantler, David Vaccari,
Bethany Knox, Craig Burns,
Tiffany Little Canfield, Stephanie Yankwitt,
Betsy Sherwood, Carrie Rosson, Justin Huff

DIALOG & VOCAL COACH...............DEBORAH HECHT

Advertising .... Serrino Coyne, Inc.
Production Photography.............................Joan Marcus
Acoustic Consultant...........Paul Scarbrough/a.'ku.stiks
Structural Engineering Consultant....................................
....Bill Gorlin, McLaren, P.C.
Immigration Counsel.........................Michael Rosenfeld
Production Travel.. Jill L. Citron
Payroll Manager................Cathy Guerra, Johnson West
Children's Tutoring ....On Location Education
....Maryanne Keller
Physical Therapy ....
.... Neuro Tour Physical Therapy, Inc./
.... Beth Frank, DPT
Medical Consultant............................Jordan Metzl, MD
Chaperone ....Robert Wilson
Assistant to Phil Collins ....Danny Gillen
Assistant to Bob Crowley ....Fred Hemminger
Press Assistant .... Matt Ross

CREDITS
Scenery by Hudson Scenic Studio, Inc., Scenic
Technologies, a division of Production Resource
Group, LLC, New Windsor, NY; Dazian Fabrics;
CMEANN Productions, Inc.; Stone Pro Rigging,

Inc. Automation by Foy Inventerprise, Inc.; Hudson Scenic Studio, Inc., Show control and scenic motion control featuring Stage Command Systems® by Scenic Technologies, a division of Production Resource Group, LLC, New Windsor, NY. Lighting equipment by PRG Lighting. Sound equipment by Masque Sound. Costumes by Donna Langman Costumes; Tricorne, inc.; DerDau; G! Willikers!; Pluma; Hochi Asiatico; Gene Mignola. Millinery provided by Rodney Gordon. Wigs provided by Ray Marston Wig Studio Ltd. Props by Paragon; Rabbit's Choice; Jauchem and Meeh; Randy Carfagno; ICBA, Inc.; John Cheech Design & Production; Camille Casaretti, Inc.; Steve Johnson; Jerard Studios, Trashin' the Camp furniture fabric by Old World Weavers, division of Stark Carpet. Special effects equipment by Jauchem & Meeh, Inc. Firearms by Boland Production Supply, Inc. Soundscape by Soundelux. Atmospheric effects equipment provided by Sunshine Scenic Studios and Aztec Stage Lighting. Acoustic drums by Pearl Drums. Rehearsal catering by Mojito Cuban Cuisine. Ricola natural herb cough drops courtesy of Ricola USA, Inc.

Makeup provided by M-A-C

TARZAN® rehearsed at Studio 2, Steiner Studios Brooklyn Navy Yard and New 42nd Street Studios

SPECIAL THANKS
James M. Nederlander; James L. Nederlander; Nick Scandalios; Herschel Waxman; Jim Boese; David Perry of the Nederlander Organization and Ojala Producciones, S.A.; Siam Productions, LLC

DISNEY THEATRICAL PRODUCTIONS
President ....Thomas Schumacher
SVP & General Manager.................................. Alan Levey
SVP, Managing Director & CFO............. David Schrader

General Management
Senior Vice President, International............. Ron Kollen
Vice President, Operations....................Dana Amendola
Vice President, Labor Relations .... Allan Frost
Vice President, Theatrical Licensing ... Steve Fickinger
Director, Human Resources........................June Heindel
Manager, Labor Relations .... Stephanie Cheek
Manager, Human Resources....................Cynthia Young
Manager, Information Systems............... Scott Benedict

Senior Computer Support Analyst ....
....Kevin A. McGuire

Production
Executive Music Producer .... Chris Montan
SVP, Creative Affairs .... Michele Steckler
Vice President, Creative Affairs................. Greg Gunter
VP, Physical Production........................John Tiggeloven
Manager, Physical Production ....Karl Chimielewski
Purchasing Manager ....Joseph Doughney
Staff Associate Designer....................... Dennis W. Moyes
Staff Associate Dramaturg .... Ken Cerniglia

Marketing
Vice President, Domestic Touring................. Jack Eldon
Vice President, New York...........................Andrew Flatt
Manager, New York....................................Michele Groner
Manager, New York.. Leslie Barrett
Website Manager .... Eric W. Kratzer
Assistant Manager, Communications ....Dana Torres

Sales
Vice President, Ticketing.............................Jerome Kane
Manager, Group Sales......................Jacob Lloyd Kimbro
Assistant Manager, Group Sales .... Juil Kim
Group Sales Representative......................Jarrid Crespo

Business and Legal Affairs
Senior Vice President .... Jonathan Olson
Vice President .... Robbin Kelley
Director .... Harry S. Gold
Attorney.. Seth Stuhl
Paralegal/Contract Administration ....Colleen Lober

Finance
Director .... Joe McClafferty
Manager, Finance ....Justin Gee
Manager, Finance ....John Fajardo
Production Accountants ..Barbara Tobin, Jodi Yaeger
Assistant Production Accountant............ Nikki Mitchell
Assistant Production Accountant...............Siu San Lee
Analyst .... Liz Jurist

Controllership
Director, Accounting...................................Leena Mathew
Manager, Accounting................................Erica McShane
Senior Analysts .... Stephanie Badie, Mila Danilevich,
.... Adrineh Ghouskassian
Analyst ....Ken Herrell

Administrative Staff
Dusty Bennett, Gregory Bonsignore, Jane Buchanan, Craig Buckley, Matthew Cronin, Cristi Finn, Christina

Fornaris, Dayle Gruet, Gregory Hanoian, Jonathan Hanson, Jay Hollenback, Connie Jasper, Kristine Lee, Kerry McGrath, Janine McGuire, Lisa Mitchell, Peter Ohsiek, Ryan Pears, Giovanna Primak, Roberta Risafi, Kisha Santiago, Lynne Schreur, David Scott

BUENA VISTA THEATRICAL MERCHANDISE, L.L.C.
Vice President .... Steven Downing
Merchandise Manager ....John F. Agati
Operations Manager ....Shawn Baker
Assistant Manager, Inventory .... Suzanne Jakel
Associate Buyer..Violeta Burlaza
Retail Supervisor ....Mark Nathman
Merchandise Assistant .... Ed Pisapia
On-site Retail Manager .... Jamie Sponcil
On-site Assistant Retail Manager......Seth Augspurger

Disney Theatrical Productions
1450 Broadway
New York, NY 10018

www.disneyonbroadway.com

ACKNOWLEDGMENTS

ONCE AGAIN I am indebted to the peerless Wendy Lefkon of Disney Editions, both for her continued faith in me as a writer and for her treasured friendship, great sense of humor, and shared birthday lunches. I am particularly grateful to Jon Glick, the excellent designer of *Tarzan*: *The Broadway Adventure* on this, our third Disney book together, for being the world's most easy-going collaborator, and to Jessie Ward of Disney Editions for so much help on this, our first project.

I'd like to thank Thomas Schumacher, president of Disney Theatrical Productions, for all his work over the twenty-five years that we've known each other and for sharing so much of it with me (and thanks, too, to Matthew White, who helps make Tom Schumacher possible while making the world a more beautiful place).

Other stalwarts at Disney Theatrical earn my continued thanks for their ongoing tolerance: Alan Levey, Marshall B. Purdy, and Michele Steckler, in particular. Gratitude and affection in equal measure go to *Tarzan* production stage manager Clifford Schwartz, the best there is, and his crack staff, especially Robby Armitage for setting up all those interviews with the cast!

I owe special thanks to company manager Randy Meyer and his associate, Eduardo Castro, for much assistance at Steiner Studios and at the Richard Rodgers.

Brian Webb and Richard Swan went above and beyond the responsibilities of their job descriptions to help with the images from the show. And while we're at it, thanks to the inimitable Joan Marcus, shutterbug and Broadway baby, who shoots from the hip and is always a hoot to watch in action.

This book would not have been possible without the very generous assistance of Mr. Danton Burroughs, grandson of Edgar Rice Burroughs, who opened the family archive for us. We also want to thank Sandra Galfas, president of Edgar Rice Burroughs, Inc., for her help with the historic photographs and other matters, and Cathy Wilbanks, also from ERB, Inc., for her invaluable assistance. For the best online source of material on Tarzan® and the Burroughs family, go to www.tarzan.org.

For kindnesses and courtesies large and small, I'd like to thank Dusty Bennett, Ken Cerniglia, Lizz Cone, Greg Gunter, Fred Hemminger, Jeff Lee, and Seth Stuhl; also Steven Downing for the souvenir program gig, not to mention Dana Torres, for her meticulously detailed attention to the *Playbill/Showbill* pieces; and I'd be remiss not to acknowledge Chris Boneau of Boneau/Bryan-Brown and his energetic staff for backup material and for keeping me in the loop.

Everyone in the *Tarzan* cast and company deserves at least one kiss for putting up with my nosy presence, particularly Bob Crowley, who was never too busy to talk, and to Phil Collins for his amiable availability—they are both worthy role models to anyone with aspirations.

I much appreciate the time spent with Kara Madrid, Whitney Osentoski, Niki Scalera, Natalie Silverlieb, and Rachel Stern, from the hard-working *Tarzan* ensemble. And thanks, especially to Angela Philiips and Leonora Stapleton, who deserve special mention for having been such fun to sit next to at the first *Tarzan* rehearsal, and for their hugs and smiles at so many rehearsals after.

I'd also like to offer a shout-out, as they say, to Timothy Pettolina, house manager of the Richard Rodgers Theater, and his staff, for their indulgent hospitality—especially the upstairs ushers who were displaced every time I did an interview while they were trying to stuff their *Playbills*.

I would like to extend special thanks to Donna Warner, editor-in-chief of *Metropolitan Home*, and the entire staff for making it possible for me to do this.

Ben Mah, the most patient man in the world, deserves to be thanked all the time whether there's a reason or not.

And I would like especially to thank my father, for his love of theater and of his family; the staff of Winthrop Hospital in Mineola, New York, for everything they did for him; my cousins for their constant support; and especially my mother for many reasons, but in particular for her strength and devotion during my father's illness.

It takes a village…!

Michael Lassell, New York City